THE PARTICULAR CLASSICS SERIES

Glory of a True Church

BENJAMIN KEACH

1640 - 1704

Keach, Rev. Benjamin, was born in Stokeham, England, Feb. 29, 1640. He found peace through Christ in his fifteenth year; and being unable to discover infant baptism or baptism by sprinkling in the Bible, and being fully satisfied that every believer should be immersed, he was baptized after the Saviour's example by John Russel, and united with a neighboring Baptist church....Mr. Keach was a zealous Baptist; he aided ministers who came to him from all parts of his country, he had many meeting-houses built, and his works in defense of Baptist principles were read all over the kingdom. Before his death men spoke of him as the "famous" Mr. Keach, and he is still described by writers as a man of great celebrity....He died July 18, 1704, in his sixty-fourth year. He was a devout Christian who led a blameless life and died in the triumphs of faith.

—William Cathcart, *The Baptist Encyclopedia*, (Philadelphia: L. H. Everts, 1881), 637-38.

the

GLORY OF A TRUE CHURCH

BENJAMIN KEACH

MATTHEW 18:18
Whatsoever ye shall bind on earth shall be bound in heaven:
and whatsoever ye shall loose on earth shall be loosed in heaven.

EDITED BY
QUINN R. MOSIER

BAPTIST HERITAGE PRESS
KANSAS CITY, MO

THE
GLORY
OF A
TRUE CHURCH,

And its

Discipline display'd.

Wherein a true Gospel-Church is described.

Together with the Power of the Keys, and who are to be let in, and who to be shut out.

By *BENJAMIN KEACH*.

Mat. 18. 18. *Whatsoever ye shall bind on Earth, shall be bound in Heaven; and whatsoever ye shall loose on Earth, shall be loosed in Heaven.*

LONDON;
Printed in the Year 1697.

BAPTIST HERITAGE

PRESS

www.baptistheritagepress.org

First published 1697
Copyright © 2022 Baptist Heritage Press
All rights reserved.

Typeset in Minion Pro at
Baptist Heritage Press, Kansas City

CONTENTS

Series Preface i
Editor's Preface v
Letter to the Reader xi

Part One
THE GLORY OF A GOSPEL-CHURCH, AND THE TRUE ORDERLY DISCIPLINE THEREOF EXPLAINED

1. Concerning a True and Orderly Gospel-Church	1
Of the Work of a Pastor, Bishop, or Overseer	3
The Office and Work of Deacons	5
Of the Duty of Church Members to Their Pastor	5
Of the Reception of Members	10
2. The Power of the Keys, With Church Discipline and Members' Duties One to Another	13
Of Church Censure	15
Of Private Offences of One Brother Against Another	17
Of Scandalous Persons Guilty of Gross Acts of Immorality	20
Of Dealing With Heretics and Blasphemers	21
Of Such That Cause Divisions or Unduly Separate Themselves From the Church	27
Of Disorders, or Causes of Discords, and How to Be Prevented, Corrected, and Removed	31
What Tends to the Glory and Beauty of a True Gospel-Church	37
The Conclusion	43

Part Two
THE SOLEMN COVENANT OF THE CHURCH OF CHRIST MEETING IN WHITESTREET, AT ITS CONSTITUTION

3. The Solemn Covenant	51

THE ARTICLES OF FAITH OF THE CHURCH OF CHRIST MEETING AT HORSLEY-DOWN

The Epistle to the Congregation	57
The Articles of Faith	61

INDEXES

Scripture Index	92

THE PARTICULAR CLASSICS SERIES

Series Preface

he *Particular Classics Series* aims to introduce the laity, pastor, and scholar to the classic works of the Particular Baptists. The works included in the series have been carefully selected to both reflect the best of the literature, as well as recover works that have largely been forgotten and/or never republished. It is our hope that these selected works will whet the appetite and summon Baptists to take up and read, to discover our Baptist fathers, and recover a heritage that has been buried for far too long.

One reason I am convinced names like Keach, Collins, Knollys, Coxe, and others do not live on in the hearts of their offspring is because their works are simply inaccessible. If a brave soul does track down a digital scan of one of these books, they will soon discover that it is a product from the Old World, a different world, with odd spellings and long S's that are taxing on modern eyes. The *Particular Classics Series* aims to not only make these works accessible, but aesthetically pleasing and enjoyable to read. These works are apples of gold, and it is a shame if they be not carried in baskets of silver.

To facilitate ease of reading and understanding, the following editorial actions have been made:

1. For uniformity, spelling has been updated to modern standards. For example, words like "satisfie" are changed to "satisfy", "knowledg" to "knowledge", and "ceas'd" to "ceased." While the spelling is updated, *the original wording of the author is still preserved.*

2. Capitalization has been removed from non-proper nouns.

3. Unnecessary italics have been removed. Typically, italics were used in place of quotation marks for Scripture. All italics have been removed and replaced with quotation marks, except for those deemed by the editor to be original to the author's intent of drawing emphasis to a particular word or phrase.

4. Punctuation has been updated to remove excess commas and replace colons and semi-colons with periods or commas where appropriate. At times, the grammar has been slightly modified to better recover the meaning of the author. If a word is missing in the original manuscript so as to make the sentence incomplete (which is not uncommon), the editor has supplied the missing words in brackets ([…]).

5. The original footnotes have been kept. Editorial footnotes are provided in square brackets ([…]) to add more detail to citations, provide uncited Scripture references, or other helpful aid.

6. Paragraph divisions have been made by the editor when deemed necessary to break up a long paragraph. These divisions have been done with care to ensure that units of thought original to the author are kept intact.

7. The original authors used copious amounts of divisions and subdivisions for a topic under consideration. The numerals

employed often become confused, incomplete, or even at times inaccurate. Care has been taken to rectify these errors by using the following gradation of numerals—1, (1), [a], first, and *first.*

8. Chapter and headings have been added to help aid the reader. When possible, these headings are taken by the author himself, but in some cases they have been crafted by the editor to facilitate ease of reading.

9. For uniformity, all quoted Scripture passages conform to the King James Version (matching the 1987 printing), unless it is obvious the original author is working with the Greek and Hebrew to support a point. The Particular Baptists used the Great Bible, the Geneva Bible, and the King James Bible. Those who had university training often examined the Greek and Hebrew.

In all editorial decisions, I have been cautious rather than assertive. Like an archaeologist delicately brushing off the dirt to preserve antiquity buried underneath the surface, so I have sought merely to brush off the dirt rather than shovel carelessly.

To quote Benjamin Keach, "I shall not therefore retain thee longer at the door." Enter the door and see for yourself the grand mansion our Baptist fathers left us. Be no longer an orphan, but come and listen to the voices of the past. In a new age when so many side trails tempt us, continue walking in the ancient paths our brave forefathers have trod before us.

QUINN R. MOSIER
Kansas City, MO
Soli Deo Gloria

Editor's Preface

 have taken the editorial liberty of combining two separately published works into one for this volume. *The Glory of a True Church* (1697) originally only contains Keach's writing on what constitutes an orderly gospel-church and the solemn covenant of Horsleydown Church from 1696. I have added to the end of this reprinting, *The Articles of the Faith of the Church of Christ, or, Congregation Meeting at Horsley-down* (1697), published in the same year as *Glory of a True Church*.

My intention in doing so is to present in one volume Keach's teaching on church polity, combined with both Horsleydown's church covenant and statement of faith.

QM

the

GLORY OF A TRUE CHURCH

and its discipline displayed

To the baptized churches,
particularly to that under my care

Letter to the Reader

My Brethren,

Every house or building consisteth both of matter and form, and so doth the church of Christ, or house of the living God.

The matter, or materials, with which it is built are *lively stones,* that is, converted persons. Also the matter and form must be according to the rule and pattern shewed in the mount; I mean Christ's institution and the apostolical churches constitution, and not after men's inventions.

Now some men, because the typical church of the Jews was national and took in their carnal seed, as such, therefore the same matter and form they would have under the gospel.

But though a church be rightly built in both these respects, that is, of fit matter and right form, yet without a regular and orderly discipline it will soon lose its beauty and be polluted.

Many reverend divines of the Congregational way have written most excellently, it is true, upon this subject; I mean on church discipline. But the books are so voluminous that the poorer sort can't purchase them, and many others have not time or learning enough to improve them to their profit. And our brethren, the Baptists, have not written, as I can gather, on this subject by itself.

Therefore, I have been earnestly desired by our members, and also by one of our pastors, to write a small and plain tract concerning the rules of the discipline of a gospel church, that all men may not only know our faith, but see our order in this case also. True, this though plain is but short, but maybe it may provoke some other person to do it more fully. Certainly, ignorance of the rules of discipline causes no small trouble and disorders in our churches, and if this may be a prevention, or prove profitable to any, let God have the glory and I have my end,

Who am yours,
BENJAMIN KEACH
August 1697

Part One

The Glory of a Gospel-Church,
And the True Orderly Discipline Thereof Explained

1

Concerning a True and Orderly Gospel-Church

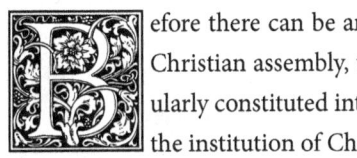efore there can be any orderly discipline among a Christian assembly, they must be orderly and regularly constituted into a church-state, according to the institution of Christ in the gospel.

1. A church of Christ, according to the gospel institution, is a congregation of godly Christians, who as a stated assembly, being first baptized upon the profession of faith, do by mutual agreement and consent give themselves up to the Lord and one to another, according to the will of God, and do ordinarily meet together in one place for the public service and worship of God, among whom the word of God and sacraments are duly administered, according to Christ's institution.[1]

2. The beauty and glory of which [a] congregation doth consist in [is] their being all converted persons, or "lively stones," being by the Holy Spirit united to Jesus Christ, the precious cornerstone and only foundation of every Christian, as well as of

---

[1] Acts 2:41–44; 5:13–14; 8:14; 19:4–6; Rom. 6:17; Eph. 1:1–2; 2:12–13, 19; Col. 1:2, 4, 12; Heb. 6:1–2; 1 Pet. 2:5.

every particular congregation and of the whole catholic church.[2]

3. That every person before they are admitted members in such a church so constituted must declare to the church, or to such with the pastor that they shall appoint, what God hath done for their souls, or their experiences of a saving work of grace upon their hearts. And also the church should enquire after, and take full satisfaction concerning, their holy lives or good conversations.[3]

And when admitted members, before the church they must solemnly enter into a covenant to walk in the fellowship of that particular congregation, and submit themselves to the care and discipline thereof,[4] and to walk faithfully with God in all his holy ordinances, and there to be fed and have communion, and worship God there when the church meets, if possible, and give themselves up to the watch and charge of the pastor and ministry thereof.[5] The pastor, then, also signifies in the name of the church their acceptance of each person, and endeavour to take the care of them, and to watch over them in the Lord, the members being first satisfied to receive them and to have communion with them. And so, the pastor [is] to give them the right hand of fellowship of a church, or *church organical*.

A church, thus constituted, ought forthwith to choose them a pastor, elder or elders, and deacons, we reading of no other officers or offices abiding in the church. And what kind of men they

---

[2] Eph. 2:20–21; Col. 2:19; Rom. 6:3–5; 1 Pet. 2:4–6.

[3] Psa. 66:16; Jer. 50:5; Acts 11:4–24; 2 Cor. 8:5; 1 Pet. 3:15.

[4] Heb. 13:17.

[5] 1 Pet. 5:1–2.

ought to be, and how qualified, is laid down by Paul to Timothy and to Titus.[6] Moreover, they are to take special care that both bishops, overseers, or elders, as well as the deacons, have in some competent manner all those qualifications. And after in a day of solemn prayer and fasting that they have elected them, whether pastor, *etc.*, or deacons, and they accepting, the office must be ordained with prayer and laying on of hands of the eldership, being first proved and found meet and fit persons for so sacred an office.[7] Therefore, such are very disorderly churches who have no pastor or pastors ordained, they acting not according to the rule of the gospel, having something wanting.

OF THE WORK OF A PASTOR, BISHOP, OR OVERSEER

1. The work of a pastor is to preach the word of Christ, or to feed the flock,[8] and to administer all the ordinances of the gospel which belong to his sacred office,[9] and to be faithful and laborious therein, studying to shew himself approved unto God, "a workman that needeth not to be ashamed, rightly dividing the word of truth."[10] He is "a steward of the mysteries of God."[11] Therefore, [he] ought to be a man of good understanding and experience, being sound in the faith, and one that is acquainted with the mysteries of the gospel because he is to feed the people

---

[6] 1 Tim. 3:2–7; Tit. 1:5–10.

[7] Acts 6:6; 1 Tim. 5:22; Tit. 1:7.

[8] 1 Cor. 9:16–17.

[9] Acts 20:31, 35.

[10] 2 Tim. 2:15.

[11] 1 Cor. 4:1–2; 1 Tim. 3.

with "knowledge and understanding."[12] He must be faithful and skillful to declare the mind of God, and diligent therein also to preach "in season and out of season,"[13] God having committed unto him the ministry of reconciliation,[14] a most choice and sacred trust. What interest hath God greater in the world which he hath committed unto men than this? Moreover, he must make known the whole counsel of God to the people.[15]

2. A pastor is to visit his flock, to know their state, and to watch over them, to support the weak, and to strengthen the feeble-minded, and succour the tempted, and to reprove them that are unruly.[16]

3. To pray for them at all times, and with them, also when sent for and desired and as opportunity serves, and to sympathize with them in every state and condition, with all love and compassion.

4. And to shew them in all respects, as near as he can, a good example "in conversation, in charity, in spirit, in faith, in purity"[17] that his ministry may be the more acceptable to all, and the name of God be glorified, and religion delivered from reproach.

5. He must see he carries it to all with all impartiality, not preferring the rich above the poor, nor lording it over God's heritage, nor assuming any greater power than God hath given him,

---

[12] Jer. 3:15.

[13] 2 Tim. 4:2.

[14] 2 Cor. 5:18.

[15] Acts 20:20, 27.

[16] Prov. 27:23; 1 Thess. 5:15; [1 Thess. 5:14].

[17] 1 Tim. 4:12.

but to shew a humble and meek spirit, nay to be "clothed with humility."[18]

THE OFFICE AND WORK OF DEACONS

The work of deacons is to serve tables, namely to see to provide for the Lord's table, the minister's table, and the poor's table.[19] First, they should provide bread and wine for the Lord's table. Second, see that every member contributes to the maintenance of the ministry according to their ability and their own voluntary subscription or obligation.[20] Third, that each member do give weekly to the poor as God has blessed him. Fourth, also visit the poor and know their condition as much as in them lies that none, especially the aged widows, be neglected.[21]

OF THE DUTY OF CHURCH MEMBERS TO THEIR PASTOR

First, 'tis the duty of every member to pray for their pastor and teachers. "Brethren, pray for us, that the word of the Lord may run and be glorified."[22] Again, saith Paul, "Praying also for us, that God would open unto us a door of utterance, to speak the mystery of Christ."[23] Prayer was made without ceasing of the church unto God for him. They that neglect this duty seem not to care either for their minister, or their own souls, or whether

---

[18] Jas. 2:4; 1 Tim. 5:21; 1 Pet. 5:3–6.

[19] Acts 6:1–10; 5:7–10.

[20] 1 Cor. 16:2.

[21] Acts 6:1.

[22] [2 Thess. 3:1]; 1 Thess. 5:25.

[23] [Col. 4:3]; Heb. 13:18.

sinners be converted, and the church edified or not. They pray for their daily bread, and will they not pray to have the bread of life plentifully broken to them?

Motives to This

1. [The] minister's work is great. "Who is sufficient for these things?"[24]

2. The opposition is not small which is made against them.[25]

3. God's loud call is, as well as ministers themselves, for the saints' continual prayers and supplication for them.[26]

4. Their weakness and temptations are many.

5. The increase and edification of the church depends upon the success of their ministry.

6. If they fall or miscarry, God is greatly dishonoured and his ways and people reproached.

Secondly, they ought to shew a reverential estimation of them, being Christ's ambassadors, also called rulers, angels, *etc.*[27] They that honour them and receive them, honour and receive Jesus Christ. "Esteem them very highly in love for their work's sake."[28] Again, he saith, "Let the elders that rule well be accounted worthy of double honour, especially they who labour in the word and

---

[24] 2 Cor. 2:16.

[25] 1 Cor. 16:9.

[26] 1 Tim. 4:3–5.

[27] 2 Cor. 5:19–20.

[28] 1 Thess. 5:13.

doctrine."[29] That is, as I conceive, such that are most laborious.

Thirdly, 'tis their duty to submit themselves unto them, that is in all their exhortations, good counsels, and reproofs. And when they call to any extraordinary duty as prayer, fasting, or days of thanksgiving, if they see no just cause why such days should not be kept, they ought to obey their pastor or elder as in other cases also. "Obey them that have the rule over you, and submit yourselves."[30]

Fourthly, it is their duty to take care to vindicate them from the unjust charges of evil men or tongue of infamy, and not to take up a reproach against them by report, nor to grieve their spirits or weaken their hands.[31]

Fifthly, 'tis the duty of members to go to them when under trouble or temptations.

Sixthly, it is their duty to provide a comfortable maintenance for them and their families suitable to their state and condition. "Let him that is taught in the word communicate unto him that teacheth in all good things."[32] "Who goeth a warfare any time at his own charges? who planteth a vineyard, and eateth not of the fruit thereof? *etc.*"[33] "Even so hath the Lord ordained that they which preach the gospel should live of the gospel."[34] "If we have sown unto you spiritual things, *is it* a great thing if we shall reap

[29] 1 Tim. 5:17.

[30] Heb. 13:5, 17.

[31] Jer. 20:10; Zeph. 2:8; 2 Cor. 11:21, 23.

[32] Gal. 6:6.

[33] 1 Cor. 9:7–8.

[34] 1 Cor. 9:14.

your carnal things?"[35] They should minister to them cheerfully with all readiness of mind.[36] Ministers are not to ask for their bread, but to receive it honourably. The minister's maintenance, though it is not by tithes, *etc.*, as under the law, yet they have now as just a right to a comfortable maintenance as they had then; the equity of the duty is the same. "Our Saviour," saith Dr. Owen, "and the apostles plead it out from grounds of equity and justice, and all kind of laws and rules of righteousness, among all sorts of men."[37]

Seventhly, it is their duty to adhere to them and abide by them in all their trials and persecutions for the word. "Ye were not ashamed of me in my bonds, *etc*."[38]

Eighthly, Dr. Owen adds another duty of the members to their pastor, namely to agree to come together upon his appointment.[39] "When they were come, and had gathered the church together, *etc*."[40]

---

[35] 1 Cor. 9:11.

[36] Matt. 10:9–10.

[37] See Dr. Owen's Eshod, p. 21–22. [Citation from John Owen, "Eshcol: A Cluster of the Fruit of Canaan," in *The Works of John Owen,* vol. 13, ed. William H. Goold (New York: Robert Carter & Brothers, 1852), 60.]

[38] 2 Tim. 4:16–18.

[39] Eshod, 27 [cf. Rule 7 in Owen, "Eshcol," in *The Works of John Owen*, vol. 13, 61–62.]

[40] Acts 14:27.

QUESTION
Are there no ruling elders besides the pastor?

ANSWER. There might be such in the primitive apostolical church, but we see no ground to believe it an abiding office to continue in the church, but was only temporary.

1. Because we have none of the qualifications of such elders mentioned, or how to be chosen.

2. Because we read not particularly what their work and business is or how distinct from preaching elders, though we see not but the church may, if she sees meet, choose some able and discreet brethren to be helps in government.[41] We have the qualifications of bishops and deacons directly laid down,[42] and how to be chosen, and their work declared,[43] but of no other office or officers in the church but these only.

QUESTION
May an elder of one church, if called, warrantably administer all ordinances to another?

ANSWER. No, surely.[44] For we find no warrant for any such practice, he being only ordained pastor or elder of that particular church that chose him,[45] *etc.*, and hath no right or authority to

[41] Rom. 12:8.

[42] 1 Tim. 3.

[43] Tit. 1:5–7.

[44] Acts 20:17, 27–28.

[45] Tit. 1:5; 1 Cor. 14:40; 1 Tim. 3.

administer, as an elder, in any other where he is not so much as a member.

QUESTION

May a church call out a teacher that is no ordained elder to administer all ordinances to them?

Answer. You may as well ask, "May a church act disorderly?" Why were ministers to be ordained if others unordained might warrantably do all their work? If therefore they have no person fitly qualified for that office, they must look out from abroad for one that is. Yet, as we say, necessity has no law. Provided therefore they can't do either, it is better their teacher be called to do it than that the church should be without their food and church ordinances neglected. Yet, let all churches take care to organize themselves, and not through covetousness, or neglect of duty, rest incomplete churches, and so under sin. "God is not *the author* of confusion, but of peace, as in all churches of the saints."[46] And how severely did God deal of old with such that meddled with the priest's work and office who were not of the priesthood, nor called by him to administer in holy things!

OF THE RECEPTION OF MEMBERS
QUESTION
What is the order of receiving members into the church that were no members anywhere before?

---

[46] 1 Cor. 14:33, 38.

Answer. The person must give an account of his faith,[47] and of the work of grace upon his soul before the church,[48] and also a strict inquiry must be made about his life and conversation.[49] But if through bashfulness the party cannot speak before the congregation, the elder and two or three more persons may receive an account of his or her faith and report it to the church.[50] But if full satisfaction by the testimony of good and credible persons is not given of the party's life and conversation, he must be put by until satisfaction is obtained in that respect.[51] Moreover, when the majority are satisfied, and yet one or two persons are not, the church and elder will do well to wait a little time and endeavour to satisfy such persons, especially if the reasons of their dissent seem weighty.

QUESTION

What is to be done when a person offers himself for communion from a church that is corrupt or erroneous in principles?

Answer. 1. The church ought to take an account of his faith in all fundamental points and of the work of grace upon his heart.

2. And if satisfied, then to send also to that corrupt people to know whether they have anything or not against his life and conversation. If satisfied in both these respects, the church may receive him.

---

[47] Psa. 66:16.

[48] Acts 9:26–27.

[49] 3 Jn. 9–10.

[50] Rom. 14:17, 19; 15:1–2; 1 Cor. 14:40; 1 Pet. 3:15.

[51] Acts 11:2–6.

QUESTION

To whom is it members join themselves? Is it to the elder or to the church?

ANSWER. They are joined to the whole community of the church, being incorporated as members thereof, and thereto abide, though the pastor be removed by death.[52]

---

[52] Acts 2:47; 5:11, 15.

2

The Power of the Keys

with

Church Discipline and Members' Duties One to Another

We judge it necessary that a day monthly be appointed particularly for discipline, and not to manage such affairs on the Lord's Day, which should be spent in the public worship of God of a different nature. Besides, such things may, on the account of discipline, come before the church which may not be expedient to be heard on the Lord's Day, lest it disturb the spirits of any members and hinder their meditation in the word which they have newly heard. Though in small congregations, perhaps, a day in two or three months may be sufficient.

2. The power of the keys, or to receive in and shut out of the congregation, is committed unto the church.[1]

"The political power of Christ," saith Dr. Chauncy, "is in the church, whereby it is exercised in the name of Christ, having all lawful rule and government within itself," which he thus proves.

[1] Acts 16:5; 2 Thess. 1:3–6.

Namely,

>1. The church essential is the first subject of the keys.
>
>2. They must of necessity to their preservation purge from themselves pernicious members.
>
>3. They have power to organize themselves with officers. Yet, I humbly conceive I may add that the concurrence of the presbytery is needful hereunto.
>
>4. If need be that they call an officer from without, or one of another church, they must first admit him a member that they may ordain their officer from among themselves.
>
>5. They have power to reject a scandalous pastor from office and membership. This power of Christ is exerted as committed to them by the hands of the elder appointed by Christ, the due management whereof is in and with the church to be his care and trust as a steward, whereof he is accountable to Christ and the church, not lording it over God's heritage.[2]

And that the power of the keys is in the church appears to me from Matthew 18, "If he neglect to hear the church." It is not said, "If he will not hear the elder, or elders."

As also that of the apostle in directing the church to cast out the incestuous person, he doth not give this counsel to the elder or elders of the church, but to the church.[3] So he commands the

---

[2] Dr. Chauncy on the *Power of the Keys*, p. 335. [cf. Isaac Chauncy, *The Doctrine Which is according to Godliness* (London: Printed for the Author by H. Hills, 1694), 334–35.]

[3] 1 Cor. 5:4–5.

church to withdraw from every brother that walks disorderly.[4] "Purge out therefore the old leaven, that ye may be a new lump."[5]

OF CHURCH CENSURES

Now as to church censures, I understand but two besides suspension. Namely, first, withdrawing from a member that walks disorderly. Secondly, casting out, or excommunicating such that are either guilty of notorious or scandalous crimes, of heresy, *etc.*, or of contemning the authority of the church. Briefly to each of these.

1. Suspension is to be when a member falls under sin and the church wants time fully to hear the matter and so can't withdraw from him, or cast him out.

2. If any member walks disorderly, though not guilty of gross scandalous sins, he or she, as soon as it is taken notice of, ought to be admonished and endeavours to be used to bring him to repentance. "For we hear that there are some which walk among you disorderly, working not at all, but are busybodies."[6] Such as meddle with matters that concern them not, it may be, instead of following their trade and business, they go about from one member's house to another telling or carrying of tales and stories of this brother or of that brother or sister, which perhaps may be true, or perhaps false, and may be to the reproach or scandal of some member or members, which, if so, it is backbiting, and that is so notorious a crime that without repentance they shall not as-

---

[4] 2 Thess. 3:6, 14.

[5] 1 Cor. 5:7.

[6] 2 Thess. 3:11–12.

cend God's holy hill.[7] Backbiting is a diminishing our neighbour's or brother's good name, either by denying him his due praise, or by saying anything to his charge falsely, or irregularly, or without sufficient cause or evidence. Thus our annotators. But this of disorderly walking does not amount to such a crime, but evils not so notorious. "Now them that are such we command and exhort by our Lord Jesus Christ, that with quietness they work, and eat their own bread."[8] They must be admonished.

1. An admonition is a faithful endeavour to convict a person of a fault, both as to matter of fact and circumstance. And this admonition must be given first, if it be private, by that brother that knows or has knowledge of the fault or evil of the person offending, whether the elder or member. For any private brother ought to admonish such with all care and faithfulness before he proceeds farther. But if it be public, the church ought to send for the offender and the pastor must admonish him before all.

2. But if after all due endeavours used he is not reclaimed, but continues a disorderly person, the church must withdraw from him. "Now we command you, brethren, in the name of our Lord Jesus Christ, that ye withdraw yourselves from every brother that walketh disorderly, and not after the tradition he received of us."[9] This is not a delivering up to Satan, excommunicating or dismembering the person, for this sort are still to be owned as members, though disorderly ones. The church must note him so as not to have communion or company with him in that sense.

---

[7] Psa. 15:1, 3.

[8] 2 Thess. 3:12.

[9] 2 Thess. 3:6.

"Yet count him not as an enemy, but admonish him as a brother" and "If any man obey not our word…note that man."[10] It appears that such who refuse to adhere to what the pastor commands and exhorts to, in the name of Christ, are to be deemed disorderly persons, as such are who meet not with the church when assembled together to worship God,[11] or that neglect private or family prayer, or neglect their attendance on the Lord's Supper, or to contribute to the necessary charges of the church, or suffer any evils unreproved in their children. All such may be looked upon disorderly walkers and ought to be proceeded against according to this rule, or divulge the private resolves of the church, as well as in many like cases.

OF PRIVATE OFFENCES OF ONE BROTHER AGAINST ANOTHER

1. As touching private offences, the rule Matthew 18 is to be observed. Only this, by the way, must be premised, namely if but one brother or two have the knowledge of some member's crime, yet if it be publicly known to the world, and the name of God be reproached, it being an immoral act, a private brother is not to proceed with such an offender according to Matthew 18, but forthwith to bring it to the church that the public scandal may be taken off.

2. But if it be a private offence or injury done to a brother or sister in particular, and not being a notorious scandalous sin, that brother must not mention it to one soul, either within or without

---

[10] 2 Thess. 3:14–15.

[11] Heb. 10:25.

the church, until he hath proceeded according to the rule.

(1.) He must tell his brother his fault. "Moreover if thy brother shall trespass against thee, go and tell him his fault between thee and him alone: if he shall hear thee, thou hast gained thy brother."[12]

Thou must labour in love and all affections to convince him of his fault. But if he will not hear thee,

(2.) Thou must take one or two more, but be sure see they are discreet persons and such that are most likely to gain upon him, and they with thee are to labour with all wisdom to bring him to the sense of his fault. 'Tis not just to speak to him as if that were enough. No, no, but to take all due pains and to strive to convince him that so the matter may be issued and the church not troubled with it. "But if he will not hear thee, then take with thee one or two more, that in the mouth of two or three witnesses every word may be established."[13]

3. But if he will not hear them after all due means and admonitions used, then it must be brought to the church. And if he will not hear the church, he must be cast out. The elder is to put the question, whether the offending brother be in their judgments incorrigible and refuseth to hear the church, which passing in the affirmative by the vote of the congregation,[14] or the majority of the brethren by the lifting up of their hands, or by their silence, the pastor after calling upon God and opening the nature of the offence and the justness of their proceedings, in the name and by

---

[12] Matt. 18:15.

[13] Matt. 18:16.

[14] The sisters are not to vote in the church.

the authority of Christ, pronounces the sentence of excommunication to this effect.[15]

> That *A. B.* being guilty of great iniquity, and not manifesting unfeigned repentance, but refusing to hear the church, I do in the name, and by the authority of Christ committed unto me as pastor of this his church, pronounce and declare that he is to be, and is hereby excommunicated, excluded or cast out of the congregation, and no longer to be owned a brother or a member of this church, and this for the destruction of the flesh that his spirit may be saved in the day of the Lord Jesus.[16]

And this, we believe, is the substance of that which the apostle calls a delivering up to Satan, he being cast into the world, which is called the kingdom of Satan, where he rules and reigns.

"The delivery unto Satan," saith Dr. Chauncy,

> signifies only the solemn exclusion of a person from the communion of the church, the visible kingdom of Christ, and disenfranchising him, or divesting him of all visible right to church-privileges, casting him into the kingdom of the world, where the prince of darkness rules in the children of disobedience.[17]

And this being done, he is to be esteemed to be no better than an heathen man, or publican, or as an evil person, and not to

---

[15] Dr. Chauncy, p. 345. [Chauncy, *The Doctrine Which is according to Godliness*, 345.]

[16] 1 Cor. 5.

[17] Dr. Chauncy, p. 345. [Chauncy, *The Doctrine Which is according to Godliness*, 345.]

have so much as intimate civil communion withal.[18]

OF SCANDALOUS PERSONS GUILTY OF GROSS ACTS OF IMMORALITY

If any member fall into any gross acts of sin, as swearing, lying, drunkenness, fornication, covetousness, extortion, or the like, and it is known and publicly spread abroad to the great scandal and reproach of religion and of the holy name of God, his church, and people, the said offender so charged, the church must send one or two brethren to him to come before the congregation. If he will not come but doth slight and contemn the authority of the church, that will bring farther guilt upon him, for which offence he incurs the censure before mentioned. But if he doth appear, his charge is to be laid before him and the witnesses called, and after he had made his defense and said all he hath to say, and the congregation finds him guilty, then the same censure is to pass upon him to the end he may be brought to unfeigned repentance and the name of God cleared.[19] And some time must be taken to make it appear that he hath true repentance by the reformation of his life and holy walking afterwards before he be received again, and the censure of the church, in a solemn manner, be taken off.

Dr. Chauncy puts this question,[20]

> Question: *How is a church to proceed in case of open and notorious scandals?* Answer. The matter of fact, as such, being beyond all question, the church is to proceed im-

---

[18] Matt. 18:17.

[19] The church censure on notorious offenders is the same with that in Matt. 18.

[20] Pag. 343. [Chauncy, *The Doctrine Which is according to Godliness*, 343.]

mediately to censure, to vindicate the honour of Christ and his church, and to manifest to the world their just indignation against such notorious offenders, and wait for a well-grounded and tried evidence of his true repentance under that ordinance of Christ, which is appointed to that end.[21]

Observe, it is the opinion of the Doctor that though the person be penitent, yet because his sin is open and scandalous he ought to be cast out to vindicate the honour of Christ and the church as part of his just punishment, that being one reason of the ordinance of excommunication, as well as to bring the person to thorough repentance, and we are of his mind. Paul takes no notice in the case of the incestuous person of his immediate repentance, or if he repent not, then, *etc.*, but says he, "deliver such a one to Satan, *etc.*"[22] Saith the Lord, "If her father had but spit in her face, should she not be ashamed seven days? let her be shut out from the camp seven days, speaking of Miriam, and after that let her be received in again."[23]

OF DEALING WITH HERETICS AND BLASPHEMERS

As touching heretics or heresy, the same censure, when they are convicted, ought to pass against them. Heresy is commonly restrained to signify any perverse opinion or error in a fundamental point of religion, as to deny the being of God, or the deity of Christ, or his satisfaction, and justification alone by his

---

[21] 1 Tim. 5:24; Acts 5:5, 11; Jude 23; 1 Cor. 5; 2 Cor. 7:11.

[22] [1 Cor. 5:5.]

[23] Num. 12:14.

righteousness, or to deny the resurrection of the body, or eternal judgment, or the like.[24] Yet our Annotators say the word signifies the same thing with schism and divisions, which if so, such that are guilty of schism or divisions in the church ought to be excommunicated also. Heresies are called "damnable" by the apostle Peter; without repentance such cannot be saved, as "bring in damnable heresies, even denying the Lord that bought them."[25]

Two things render a man an heretic according to the common signification of the word. First, an error in matters of faith, fundamental or essential to salvation. Second, stubbornness and contumacy in holding and maintaining it. "A man that is an heretic after the first and second admonition reject."[26] Now that this rejection is all one with excommunication appears by what Paul speaks, "Of whom is Hymenaeus and Alexander; whom I have delivered unto Satan, that they may learn not to blaspheme."[27] Their heresy or blasphemy was in saying the resurrection was past.

Some would have none be counted an heretic but he who is convicted and condemned so to be in his own conscience, mistaking Paul's words, "Knowing that he that is such is subverted, and sinneth, being condemned of himself."[28] He may be condemned of himself, though not for his heresy, yet for his spend-

---

[24] See Pool's [sic] *Annot.* on 1 Cor. 11:19. [cf. Matthew Poole, *Annotations upon the Holy Bible*, vol. 3 (New York: Robert Carter and Brothers, 285, Broadway, 1852), 579.]

[25] 2 Pet. 2:1.

[26] Tit. 3:10.

[27] 1 Tim. 1:19–20.

[28] [Tit. 3:11.]

ing his time about questions and strife of words to the disquieting the peace of the church, or though not condemned of himself directly yet indirectly. According to the purport of his own notion or what he grants about the point in debate, *etc.*, else the apostle refers to some notable and notorious self-condemned heretic. It is a great question whether Hymenaeus and Alexander were condemned in their own consciences about that heresy charged upon them, and yet were delivered up to Satan. However the rule is plain respecting any that are subverted and resolutely maintain any heretical notion, i.e. after he hath been twice, or oftener, admonished, that is, after all due means used and pains taken with him to convince him of his abominable error. And yet, if he remains obstinate, he must "be delivered up to Satan," that is, the righteous censure of the church must pass upon him, as in the case of other notorious crimes. Heresy is a work of the flesh, and hence some conceive such ought to be punished by the civil magistrate.

QUESTION
What is an admonition?

Answer. It is a faithful endeavour to convict a person of a fault, both as to matter of fact and his duty thereupon, charging it on his conscience in the name of the Lord Jesus with all wisdom and authority.

QUESTION
What is a church admonition?

Answer. When an offending brother, rejecting private admonition by one or by two or three persons, the complaint being brought to the church by the elder, the offending member is rebuked and exhorted in the name of the Lord Jesus to due repentance. And if convicted and he repents, the church forgives him, otherwise casts him out as I before shewed.

QUESTION
May a church admit a member of another congregation to have communion with them without an orderly receiving him as a member?

Answer. If the person is well known by some of the church, and that he is an orderly member of a church of the same faith, he being occasionally cast among them, they may admit him to transient communion for that time. But if he abides in that town or city remote to the church to whom he belongs, he ought to have his regular dismission, and so be delivered up to the care and watch of the church where he desires to communicate.

QUESTION
If an excommunicated person hath obtained of God true repentance and desires to be restored to the church, what is the manner of his reception?

Answer. Upon his serious, solemn, and public acknowledgment thereof before the church, and due satisfaction according to the nature of his offence being given, the elder solemnly proceeds and declares in the name of the Lord Jesus that the sentence which A.B. was laid under (upon his unfeigned repentance) is taken off, and that he is received again a as member, etc., to the praise and glory of God.[29]

QUESTION

How ought a pastor to be dealt withal if he, to the knowledge of the church or any members thereof, walketh disorderly and unworthily of his sacred office and membership?

Take the answer of another author here.

> *Answer.* "Those members to whom this is manifestly known ought to go to him privately, and unknown to any others (and with the spirit of meekness, in great humility), lay his evil before him and entreat him as a father, and not rebuke him as their equal, much less as their inferior. And if they gain upon him, then to receive him into their former affection and esteem, forever hiding it from all others. But if after all tender entreaties he prove refractory and obstinate, then to bring him before the church and there to deal with him, they having two or three witnesses in the face of the church to testify matter of fact against him to their personal knowledge.
>
> 2. But before he be dealt with, they must appoint one

---

[29] Matt. 13:18; 2 Cor. 2:6–7; 1 Tim. 5.

> from among themselves qualified for the *work of* a pastor to execute the church censure against him, *etc*."[30]

Yet, no doubt, the church may suspend him from his communion and exercising of his office presently upon his being fully convicted.[31] But seeing in the multitude of counsel there is safety, surely no church would so proceed without the advice of the presbytery or of a sister church at least.

QUESTION

Suppose a member should think himself oppressed by the church or should be unjustly dealt with, either withdrawn from or excommunicated. Has he no relief left him?

ANSWER. We believe he hath relief and also that there is no church infallible but may err in some points of faith, as well as in discipline. And the way proposed and agreed to in a General Assembly held in London 1692 of the elders, ministers, and messengers of our churches we approve of, which is this, namely,

> The grieved or injured person may make his application to a sister church for communion and that church may send some brethren, in their names, to that congregation that have dealt with him, and they to see if they can possibly restore him to his place. But if they cannot, then to report the matter charged, with the proofs, to the church that sent them. And if that congregation shall, after a full information, *etc.*, be persuaded the person was not or-

---

[30] [It is unclear who Keach is citing. He does not cite his source.]

[31] I see not if they have none fitly qualified, but the church may cast him out.

derly dealt with, they may receive him into their communion.

OF SUCH THAT CAUSE DIVISIONS OR UNDULY SEPARATE THEMSELVES FROM THE CHURCH

This I find is generally asserted by all congregational divines or worthy men, that is, that no person hath power to dismember himself—that is, he cannot, without great sin, translate himself from one church to another, but ought to have a dismission from that church where he is a member,[32] provided that church is orderly constituted, nothing being wanting as to any essential of salvation or of church communion. But if not, yet he ought to endeavour to get his orderly dismission.

Nor is every small difference in some points of religion, or notions of little moment, any grounds for him to desire his dismission.

That he cannot, nor ought not, to translate himself, see what the Reverend Writer saith:

> He cannot (saith he) for many reasons:
>
> 1. It is not decent, much less orderly going away, but very unmannerly, and a kind of running away, Phil. 1:27; Tit. 2:10.
>
> 2. Such a departure is not approved of in families, or civil societies.
>
> 3. It destroys the relation of pastor and people, for what may be done by one individual, may be done by all.
>
> 4. What liberty in this kind belongs to the sheep belongs

---

[32] Rom. 6:17; Heb. 6:2–3.

also to the shepherd much more. He may then also leave his flock at his pleasure without giving notice or reason thereof to the church.

5. It is breaking covenant with Christ, and with the congregation, and therefore a great immorality, Rom. 1:31, he being under obligation to abide steadfastly with the church, i.e. till the church judge he hath a lawful call to go to another church, Acts 2:41.

6. It is a schism, for if there be any such thing in the world it's of particular societies, 1 Cor. 12:14–15, 20–21, 25; Hebrews 10:25.

7. It's a despising the government of the church., Jude 19.

8. It is a particular member assuming to himself the use of the keys, or rather stealing of them.

9. There's as much reason persons should come in when they please without asking consent, as depart when they please.

10. It is very evil, and unkind in another church to receive such an one, as not doing as they would, or should be dealt with.

11. Such practices can issue in nothing else than the breach and confusion of all particular churches, and make them like parishes.

12. Such departures cannot be pleaded for in the least, but upon he notion of a catholic visible church, wherein all members and officers are run into one organized church, which will, and must introduce, a coordinate (if not a subordinate) pastoral government (by combination

of elders) over all the churches, and therefore by synods and classes.

13. It is like a leak in a ship, which if not speedily stopped, will sink at last.

14. It tends to anarchy, putting an arbitrary power in every member.

15. It breaks all bonds of love, and raiseth the greatest animosities between brethren and churches.

16. It is a great argument of some guilt lying on the party so departing.[33]

Thus the Doctor again he saith,[34]

It is no more in the just power of a particular member to dissolve his church relation, than in a man to kill himself, but by his said withdrawment he doth schismatically rend himself from his communion...and so separate himself sinfully, Jude 19; 1 Cor. 1:10; 3:3; 11:18; Heb. 10:22–23, 25.

Question. *What is the just act of the church, that clothes this irregular separation with the formality as it were of an excommunication?*[35]

He answers calling this a mixed excommunication, that is, originally proceeding from, and consists in, "the act of the brother himself, and is the formality of his offence, upon which pro-

---

[33] Dr. Chauncy, pag. 337. [Keach cites the wrong page number. The actual citation is Chauncy, *The Doctrine Which is according to Godliness,* 339–340.]

[34] [Keach seems to embellish Chauncy's original writing here. For original, see Chauncy, *The Doctrine Which is according to Godliness,* 342.]

[35] [Ibid.]

ceeds the just and unavoidable act of the church."[36]

"The judgment of the church publicly declared by the elder of the congregation," as the Doctor words it, namely,

> That A. B., having so and so irregularly, and sinfully withdrawn…himself from the communion of the congregation, they [we] do now adjudge him a non-member, and one that is not to communicate with the church in the special ordinances of communion till due satisfaction is given by him, Rom. 16:17–18; 2 Thess. 3:6, 14–15; Jude 12.

Yet, we believe, as the Doctor's opinion is, that a church may, if they find the case to be warranted by the word of God, or as it may be circumstanced, give a dismission to a member, when insisted on, to another regular church, though not in every case of small offence or dissent in some small points of different notions, or from prejudice. For, that may tend soon to dissolve any church. For what church is it where every member is of one mind in every particular case and thing about notions of religion?[37]

And such that make divisions, and cause schisms, or discord among brethren to disturb the peace of the church, if they cannot be reclaimed, must be marked and dealt with as great *offenders*, it being one of those things that God hates and is an abomination to him.[38]

---

[36] [Chauncy, *The Doctrine Which is according to Godliness*, 342.]

[37] Let none call the church a prison, since all do voluntarily covenant with it, and 'tis dangerous to break Christ's bonds.

[38] 2 Tim. 2:23; 2 Thess. 3:14; Prov. 6:16.

QUESTION

What is a full and lawful dismission of a member to another church upon his removing his habitation, or on other warranted cases?

ANSWER. We answer, a letter testimonial or recommendation of the person. And if he intends to abide there wholly, to give him up to that communion and fellowship to be watched over in the Lord.[39]

OF DISORDERS, OR CAUSES OF DISCORDS, AND HOW TO BE PREVENTED, CORRECTED, AND REMOVED

1. One cause of discord is through the ignorance in some members of the rules of discipline and right government, particularly when that rule in Matthew 18 is not followed.[40]

But one person takes up an offence against another and speaks of it to this or that person before he hath told the brother offending of it, which is a palpable sin and a direct violation of Christ's holy precept, and such must, as offenders themselves, be in a gospel-way dealt with.

To prevent this the discipline of the church should be taught and the members informed of their duties.

2. Another thing that causes trouble and disorder in a church is want of love and tender affections to one another, as also not having a full sight and sense of the great evil of breaking "the

---

[39] Rom. 16:1–2; Acts 18:27.

[40] Matt. 18:15.

bonds of peace and unity."[41] O that all would lay this abominable evil to heart, how base a thing it is to break the peace of a private family, or neighbourhood, but much more sinful to disturb the peace of the church of the living God, and break the bonds of the unity thereof. "Behold, how good and how pleasant *it is* for brethren to dwell together in unity!"[42] But, O how ugly and hateful is the contrary![43]

3. Another disorderly practice is this: when one member or another knows of some sinful act or evils done by one or more members and they conceal it, or do not act according to the rule, pretending they would not be looked upon as contentious persons.[44] But hereby they may become guilty of other men's sins and also suffer the name of God, and the church, to lie under reproach, and all through their neglect. This is a great iniquity.

4. When an elder or church shall know that some persons are scandalous in their lives, or heretical in judgment, and yet shall bear or connive with them.

5. When members take liberty to hear at other places when the church is assembled to worship God.[45] This is nothing less than a breaking their covenant with the church and may soon dissolve any church. For by the same rule one may take that liberty, another, nay every member, may. Moreover, it casts a contempt upon the ministry of the church and tends to cause such who are

---

[41] John 13:12–17; Heb. 13:1; Eph. 4:3, 31–32; 5:2.

[42] Psa. 133:1.

[43] Jas. 3:16.

[44] Acts 5:3, 8; Lev. 19:17.

[45] Acts 4:23.

hearers to draw off and to be disaffected with the doctrine taught in the church, they knowing these dissenters do belong unto it. I exhort, therefore, in the name of Christ this may be prevented. And any of you that know who they are that take this liberty, pray discover them to the church. We lay no restraint upon our members from hearing such who are sound in the faith at other times.

6. The liberty that some take to hear men that are corrupt in their judgments, and so take in unsound notions, and also strive to distil them into the minds of others as if they were of great importance. Alas, how many are corrupted in these days with Arminianism, Socinianism, and what not! This causes great trouble and disorder.[46]

7. When one church shall receive a member or members of another congregation without their consent or knowledge. Nay, such that are disorderly and may be loose livers, or cast out for immorality, or persons filled with prejudice without cause. This is enough to make men atheists or contemn all church authority and religion. For hath not one regular church as great authority from Christ as another?

8. Another disorder is when members are received without the general consent of the church, or before good satisfaction is taken of their godly lives and conversations, or when a church is too remiss in the reception of her members.[47]

9. Another disorder is when a church shall receive a charge against a member, it being an offence between brother and brother, before an orderly proceed has been made by the offended per-

[46] 2 Pet. 2:2.
[47] Acts 9:27.

son.[48]

10. When judgment passes with partiality; some are connived at out of favor or affection. Levi was not to know his father or mother in judgment.[49]

11. When members do not constantly and early attend our public assemblies,[50] and the worship of God on the Lord's Day especially, but are remiss in that matter.[51] This is a great evil.

12. When part of a church shall meet together as dissatisfied to consult church matters without the knowledge or consent of the church or pastor. This is disorderly and tends to division, and such should be marked.[52]

13. Another thing that tends to disquiet the peace of the church is when there are any undue heats of spirit or passion shewed in the pastor or others in managing the discipline of the church.[53] Have we not found by experience the sad effect of this? Therefore things must be always managed with coolness and sweetness of spirit and moderation, every brother having liberty to speak his mind and not to be interrupted until he has done, nor above one speak at once.

14. When one brother or more dissents in the sentiments of their minds from the church in any matters circumstantial, either in respect of faith, practice, or discipline and will not submit to

[48] Matt. 18:15.
[49] [Deut. 33:8-9.]
[50] Psa. 63:1; Cant. 7:12.
[51] Mark 16:1.
[52] 1 Cor. 13:25; Rom. 16:17.
[53] 2 Tim. 2:25.

the majority, but raise feuds, nay, will rend themselves from the church, rather than consent.[54]

QUERY. What reason or ground hath any man to refuse communion with a church that Christ hath not left, but hath communion with?

15. When any member shall divulge or make known to persons not of the congregation, nor being concerned in those matters, what is done in church meetings. The church, in this respect, as well as in others, is to be as a "garden inclosed...A spring shut up, a fountain sealed."[55] This oft times occasions great grief and the disorderly person should be detected. Is it not a shame to any of a private family to divulge the secrets of the family? But far greater shame do these expose themselves unto.

16. Another disorderly practice is this, namely, when a member shall suggest and seem to insinuate into the minds of other members some evil against their pastor, yet will not declare what it is and may only be evil surmisings and out of prejudice, and yet refuses to acquaint the pastor with what it is. This is very abominable and a palpable violation of the rule of the gospel, and duty of members to their minister. Such a person ought to be severely rebuked, and if he confess not his evils, and manifesteth unfeigned repentance, to be dealt with farther. Moreover, it is a great evil in another to hear such base insinuations and neither rebuke the accuser, and so discharge his duty, nor take two or three more to bring the person to repentance. If he deals thus by a private brother, it is a great evil. But far worse to an elder, whose

[54] Jude 19; Jas. 3:14–16.

[55] Cant. 4:12.

name and honour ought with all care and justice to be kept up as being more sacred.[56]

17. Another disorderly practice is, which causes much trouble, when the public charges of a church are not equally borne, but some too much burdened when others do but little or nothing.[57]

And also, when everyone does not contribute to the poor, as God has blessed them, on every Lord's Day, or first day of the week, as he hath commanded.[58]

18. Another disorder is this: when members refuse to communicate with the church at the Lord's table because some person, or persons, they think are guilty of evil, and yet they have not proceeded with them according to rule. These either excommunicate the church, or themselves, or those persons at least they censure unwarrantably.[59]

I beseech you, for Christ's sake, that this may never be any more among you. You ought not to deal thus with them, or refuse your communion, though faulty, until the church has dismembered, or withdrawn from them, or at least suspended them.

19. When one member shall believe, or receive a report, against another before he knows the truth of the matter.[60]

20. When an accusation is brought against an elder contrary to the rule, which ought not be without two or three witnesses, as

---

[56] Rom. 1:29; 1 Tim. 6:4; Zech. 7:10; 1 Tim. 5:19.

[57] 2 Cor. 8:14.

[58] 1 Cor. 16:2.

[59] Matt. 18.

[60] Jer. 20:10.

to the matter of fact.[61]

21. When the word of God is not carefully attended upon on week or lecture days by the members generally, though the said meeting being appointed by the whole church.[62]

22. When days of prayer and fasting and of public thanksgiving, or when days of disciplining are not generally attended upon.[63]

23. Lastly, when gifted brethren are not duly encouraged, first privately, to exercise their gifts, and being in time approved, called forth to preach, or exercise in the church. And when encouragement is not given to bestow learning also upon them for their better accomplishment. What will become of the churches in time to come if this be not prevented with speed?

WHAT TENDS TO THE GLORY AND BEAUTY OF A TRUE GOSPEL-CHURCH

1. That which primarily tends to the glory of a church is the foundation on which it is built, which is Jesus Christ.[64] Now this is a blessed and glorious foundation.

First, in respect of God the Father, who laid this foundation in his eternal purpose, counsel, and decree. "Behold I lay in Zion," and this is as the result of his infinite wisdom, love, and mercy to his elect.[65]

[61] 1 Tim. 5:19.
[62] Isa. 55:3; Acts 2:1–2; 10:33.
[63] Joel 2:16.
[64] 1 Cor. 3:4.
[65] Isa. 28:16.

2. In respect had unto Christ himself, who is this foundation.

First, he is a suitable foundation. In respect to the glory of God in all his attributes.

Second, in respect to our good, he answering all our wants who are united to him or built upon him.

Third, in respect of the preciousness of Christ as a foundation, a stone, a *precious* stone.

Fourth, in respect to the durableness of it, that is, "a tried stone…a sure foundation."

Brethren, a foundation of a house must of necessity be laid. No house can be built without a good foundation that will stand firm and unmovable. It is the strongest part of the building and it beareth all the weight of the whole superstructure. So doth Jesus Christ.

3. The beauty and glory of a true church consists in the true and regular or right constitution of it, nothing being wanting that is essential to it upon this account.

4. It consisteth in the excellency, glory, and suitableness of the materials 'tis built with, answering to the foundation. All precious stones, lively stones, all regenerated persons.[66]

5. In that all the stones be well hewed and squared, all made fit for the building before laid in. Were it thus, there would not be so great a noise of the hammer and axe in church discipline, as indeed there is. It was not thus in the type—I mean in Solomon's temple.[67]

6. Its beauty and glory consisteth in that all the stones being

---

[66] 1 Pet. 2:5–6.

[67] 1 Kgs. 6:7.

not only united by the Spirit to Christ the foundation, but also to one another in sincere love and affection. "In whom all the building fitly framed together groweth up unto an holy temple in the Lord."[68]

7. It consisteth in the holiness and purity of the lives and conversations of all the members. "Be ye holy; for I am holy."[69] "Holiness becometh thine house, O LORD, for ever."[70]

8. It consisteth in that sweet union and concord that ought to be in the church, all like the horse in Pharoah's chariot, drawing together, "endeavouring to keep the unity of the Spirit in the bond of peace."[71] "By this shall all *men* know ye are my disciples, if ye have love one to another."[72]

9. In their having the divine presence with them, or when the glory of God fills his temple.[73]

10. In keeping out all unsanctified or unclean persons, or if they get in to purge them out by a strict and holy discipline, or else it will soon lose its beauty.[74]

11. In that zeal and equality that should be shewed in all to keep up the honour, peace, and comfort of the church, and the ministry thereof.[75]

---

[68] Eph. 2:19–21.
[69] 1 Pet. 1:16.
[70] Psa. 93:5.
[71] Cant. 1:9; Eph. 4:3.
[72] [John 13:35.]
[73] Exod. 20:24; Matt. 18:20.
[74] 1 Cor. 5:5–7.
[75] 2 Cor. 8:14; Tit. 3:2.

12. Firstly, in the administration of right discipline, to see no neglect nor delaying of justice through carelessness or partiality. (a.) No ways partaking of other men's sins, which may be done by conniving at it. (b.) By lessening or extenuating of it. (c.) By countenancing or any ways encouraging any in sin. (d.) By not restoring a brother that confesses his sin when overtaken. (e.) Not bringing in a just charge against an offender, nor rebuking him, and yet having communion with him.

Secondly, not to wrest judgment out of its true and right channel, nor to inflict a greater censure than the law of Christ requires on any.

Thirdly, timely to acquit and discharge a penitent person.

Fourthly, not to do anything out of prejudice, but in love and bowels of affection, and to do all in Christ's name, or by his authority.

13. To sympathize with the afflicted, succour the tempted, and relieve the poor and distressed—rejoicing with them that rejoice and mourning with them that mourn.

14. "To speak evil of no man."[76] Not only speaking no evil of their brethren, but of no man, to his hurt or injury, detracting from his worth and honour. See Sirach, "Whether it be to friend or foe, talk not of other men's lives; and if thou canst without offence, reveal them not."[77] We must not discourse his faults, unless in a gospel-way. And that too, to amend the person, and not out of passion or prejudice to expose him, but out of love to his

---

[76] [Tit. 3:2.]

[77] Ecc. 19:8. Apoc. [i.e. Ecclesiasticus 19:8, from Jesus the son of Sirach in the Apocrypha.]

soul. Yet, we may speak of the evils of others. (a.) When called to do it in a legal or gospel-way, and it is a sin then to conceal his crime. (b.) Or when it is to prevent another who is in danger to be infected by his company or ill example. (c.) Or in our own just defense and vindication. Moreover, consider the evil of reproaching of others.

First, as to the causes why some do it.

> 1. One cause is from want of love. Nay, from malice and hatred.
>
> 2. From the baseness, ill nature, and cruelty of the accuser's disposition.
>
> 3. 'Tis occasioned from that itch of talking and meddling in the affairs of other men.
>
> 4. Or perhaps to raise their own esteem and honour, some degrade their brother, which is abominable.

Consider, it is theft or robbery, nay, and 'tis worse than to rob a man of his goods, because thou takest away that which, perhaps, thou canst not restore again.

Moreover, consider that such who reproach others lay themselves open thereby to reproach.

Moreover, know he that receives or hearkens to the scandal is as guilty as the *accuser*. He is like a person that receives stolen goods, and so is as bad as the thief.

This being one of the grand and notorious evils of these days, I speak the more to it.

Second, if you abominate this evil, and avoid it, you will shine in *grace* and *virtue* the more clearly.

Alas, in our days some that would be thought to be great professors stick not to vilify Christ's ministers, even some of the best of men, and are so full of malice they care not what wrong they do to their brethren, nor to the truth itself, or interest of God, and so expose themselves to a lasting shame, and their spirit and practice to an abhorrence.[78] They are like cursed Ham who discovered his father's nakedness.[79] These persons violate all laws, both human and divine.

Third, when they bear one another's burdens, "and so fulfil the law of Christ."[80] And that you may do this, consider where is that church in which there are no burdens to be borne.

Motives Thus to Do

1. Consider what a burden Jesus Christ hath borne for thee.
2. What a burden thou hast to bear of thine own.[81]
3. Mayest not thou in some things be a burden to thy brethren?
4. Wouldst thou not have others bear thy burden?
5. May not God cause thee to bear a more heavy burden because thou canst not bear thy brother's?
6. 'Tis a fulfilling the law of love, nay the law of Christ.[82]

15. The glory and beauty of a congregation is the more manifest when the authority of the church and the dignity of the pas-

---

[78] 3 Jn. 9–10.
[79] Gen. 9:22.
[80] Gal. 6:2.
[81] Gal. 6:4.
[82] Rom. 13:10.

toral office is maintained. How great was the evil of the gainsaying of Korah? The apostles speaks of some that are self-willed, presumptuous, who are not afraid to speak evil of dignities.[83]

God has put a glory and high dignity upon the church and in its authority and power. "Whom ye bind on earth shall be bound in heaven."[84]

Moreover, the pastoral office is an office of dignity. They are called rulers, angels, fathers.[85] For any, therefore, to cast contempt on the church or pastor is a great evil and a reproach to Christ, and tends to disorder and confusion.

Lastly, when holiness, righteousness, charity, humility, and all true piety is pressed upon the consciences of every member and appears in the minister. Also, that all strive to excel therein with their uttermost care and diligences.[86]

THE CONCLUSION

Know, my brethren, that God "loveth the gates of Zion more than all the dwelling places of Jacob."[87] Therefore, the public worship of God ought to be preferred before private.

1. This supposeth there must be a visible church.

2. And that they frequently meet together to worship God.

3. That they have an orderly ministry and one ordained elder, at least, to administer all public ordinances.

---

[83] Jude 11; Num. 22:7; 2 Pet. 2:10.

[84] [cf. Matt. 16:19; 18:18.]

[85] Rev. 2:1; 1 Tim. 3:5; Acts 23:5.

[86] Psa. 110:3; 1 Pet. 1:25.

[87] Psa. 87:2.

4. Moreover, that all persons have free liberty to assemble with the church and to partake of all ordinances, save those which peculiarly belong to the church, as the Lord's Supper, holy discipline, and days of prayer and fasting.[88] Then, the church of old separated themselves from all strangers.

Yet, others may attend on all other public ordinances with the church as public prayer, reading, and preaching the word, and in singing God's praises, as hath formerly been proved.[89] May others, my brethren, join in prayer with us, and not praise God with us?

But, O my brethren! let me beseech you to shew your high value and estimation for the public worship of God.

Motives Hereunto

1. Since God prefers it thus, or has so great esteem of his public worship.

2. Because he is said to dwell in Zion. It is his habitation for ever; the place where his honour dwells.[90]

3. Here God is most glorified. In his temple every one speaks of his glory.[91] "My praise *shall be* of thee in the great congregation."[92]

4. Here is most of God's gracious presence, as one observes it.

(a.) His effectual presence, "in all places where I record

---

[88] Neh. 1:2.

[89] How should sinners else be converted and the church increased?

[90] Psa. 26:8; 132:13.

[91] Psa. 29:9.

[92] [Psa. 22:25.]

my name, I will come unto thee, and I will bless thee."[93]

(b.) Here is more of his intimate presence. "Where two or three are gathered together in my name, there am I in the midst of them."[94] He walks in the midst of the "seven golden candlesticks."[95]

5. Here are the clearest manifestations of God's beauty, which made holy David desire to dwell there forever.[96] See the appearance of Christ to the churches.[97]

6. In that it is said that those that should be saved, in the apostle's days, God added unto the church.[98]

7. Here is [the] most spiritual advantage to be got. "Here the dews of Hermon fall, they descend upon the mountain of Zion. Here God commands the blessing, even life for evermore."[99] "I will abundantly bless her provision: I will satisfy her poor with bread."[100] Here David's doubt was resolved.[101]

8. Here you received your first spiritual breath, or life. Many souls are daily born to Christ. That good which is most diffusive is to be preferred, but that good which most partake of is most diffusive. "O magnify the LORD with me, and let us exalt his name

---

[93] Exod. 20:24.

[94] Matt. 18:20.

[95] Rev. 1:13.

[96] Psa. 27:4.

[97] Rev. 2–3.

[98] Acts 2:47.

[99] Psa. 133:3. [Keach seems to be reworking Psa. 133:3.]

[100] Psa. 132:15.

[101] Psa. 73:16–17; 87:5.

together." Live coals separated soon die.[102]

9. Brethren, as a worthy divine observes, the church in her public worship is the nearest resemblance of heaven, especially in singing God's praises. What esteem, also, had God's worthies of old for God's public worship? "My soul longeth, yea, even fainteth for the courts of the Lord. How amiable *are* thy tabernacles, O LORD of hosts!"[103]

10. See how the promises of God run to Zion, or to his church.[104] He will "bless thee out of Zion."[105] O let nothing discourage you in your waiting at the posts of Christ's door.[106] David desired rather to be a doorkeeper in the house of God than to dwell in the tents of wickedness.[107] Yet, nevertheless do not neglect, for the Lord's sake, private devotion, namely secret and family prayer. O pray to be fitted for public worship![108] Come out of your closets to the church! What signifies all you do in public if you are not such that keep up the worship of God in your own families?[109]

O neglect not prayer, reading, and meditation! And take care also to educate and catechize your children, and live as men and women that are dead to this world. And walk for the Lord's sake,

[102] Psa. 34:3.
[103] Psa. 84:1–2.
[104] Isa. 35.
[105] Psa. 128:5.
[106] Isa. 51:3; Prov. 8:34; Psa. 26:14.
[107] Psa. 84:10.
[108] Matt. 6:6.
[109] Jer. 10:25.

as becomes the gospel.[110]

See that zeal and knowledge go together. A good conversation and a good doctrine go together. These two together are better than one.

Brethren, he that makes the word of God his rule in whatsoever he doth, and the glory of God his end in what he doth shall have the Spirit of God to be his strength. This is like Solomon's threefold cord that will be one or it will be three. It can't be two, nor can it be broken.[111]

---

[110] Eph. 6:4; Phil. 1:27.

[111] Ecc. 4:9–13.

Part Two

The Solemn Covenant of the Church of Christ
Meeting at Whitestreet at Its Constitution

June 5, 1696

3

The Solemn Covenant

e, who desire to walk together in the fear of the Lord, do, through the assistance of his Holy Spirit, profess our deep and serious humiliation for all our transgressions. And we do also solemnly, in the presence of God, of each other, in the sense of our own unworthiness,[1] give up ourselves to the Lord in a church-state according to the apostolical constitution that he may be our God and we may be his people through the everlasting covenant of his free grace, in which alone we hope to be accepted by him through his blessed Son Jesus Christ, whom we take to be our High Priest to justify and sanctify us, and our Prophet to teach us, and to subject to him as our Lawgiver, and the King of saints, and to conform to all his holy laws and ordinances for our growth, establishment, and consolation, that we may be as a holy spouse unto him, and serve him in our generation, and wait for his second appearance as our glorious bridegroom.

Being fully satisfied in the way of church communion and the truth of grace in some good measure upon one another's spirits, we do solemnly join ourselves together in a holy union and fel-

[1] Eze. 16:6, 8; 2 Cor. 8:5; Hos. 2:23; 2 Cor. 6:16.

lowship, humbly submitting to the discipline of the gospel, and all holy duties required of people in such a spiritual relation.[2]

1. We do promise and engage to walk in all holiness, godliness, humility, and brotherly love as much as in us lieth to render our communion delightful to God, comfortable to ourselves, and lovely to the rest of the Lord's people.[3]

2. We do promise to watch over each other's conversations and not to suffer sin upon one another, so far as God shall discover it to us, or any of us, and to stir up one another to love and good works, to warn, rebuke, and admonish one another with meekness according to the rules left to us of Christ in that behalf.[4]

3. We do promise, in an especial manner, to pray for one another and for the glory and increase of this church, and for the presence of God in it, and the pouring forth of his Spirit on it, and his protection over it to his glory.[5]

4. We do promise to bear one another's burdens, to cleave to one another, and to have a fellow feeling with one another in all conditions both outward and inward as God in his providence shall cast any of us into.[6]

5. We do promise to bear with one another's weakness, failings, and infirmities with much tenderness, not discovering to any without the church, nor any within, unless according to

---

[2] Exod. 26:3–4, 6; Isa. 62:5; Psa. 122:3; Eph. 2:23; 4:16; 1 Pet. 2:5; Psa. 93:5; Isa. 55:8; Luke 1:74–75.

[3] 2 Cor. 7:1; 1 Tim. 6:11; 2 Pet. 1:6–7; Acts 20:19; Phil. 2:3; John 13:34; 15:12.

[4] 1 Pet. 1:22; Lev. 19:17; Heb. 10:24–25; 1 Thess. 5:14–15; Rom. 15.

[5] Eph. 6:18; Jas. 5:16; Col. 4:12.

[6] Gal. 6:2; Heb. 12:12; 13:31; Rom. 12:15; 2 Cor. 11:29.

Christ's rule and the order of the gospel provided in that case.[7]

6. We do promise to strive together for the truths of the gospel and purity of God's ways and ordinances, to avoid causes and causers of division, "endeavouring to keep the unity of the Spirit in the bond of peace."[8]

7. We do promise to meet together on Lord's Days, and at other times as the Lord shall give us opportunities, to serve and glorify God in the way of his worship, to edify one another and to contrive the good of the church.[9]

8. We do promise, according to our ability (or as God shall bless us with the good things of this world), to communicate to our pastor or minister, God having ordained that they that preach the gospel should live of the gospel. (And now can anything lay a greater obligation upon the conscience than this covenant? What then is the sin of such who violate it?)[10]

These, and all other gospel duties, we humbly submit unto, promising and purposing to perform not in our own strength, being conscious of our own weakness, but in the power and strength of the blessed God, whose we are and whom we desire to serve. To whom be glory now and forevermore. Amen.

---

[7] 1 Jn. 3:17–18; Gal. 6:1; 1 Thess. 5:14; Rom. 12:15; Eph. 4:31–32.

[8] Jude 3; Gal. 5:1; Tit. 3:9–10; 2 Jn. 5,10; Eph. 4:3.

[9] Heb. 3:10; 10:25; Mal. 3:16; Rom. 14:18; 15:16.

[10] 2 Cor. 9:7–13; Gal. 6:6.

THE ARTICLES OF THE FAITH

of the

CHURCH OF CHRIST MEETING AT HORSLEYDOWN

August 10, 1697

The Epistle to the Congregation

To the congregation with whom I am a member, and the unworthy overseer, who are in God the Father, and in our Lord Jesus Christ. Grace, mercy and peace be multiplied.

Most Dear and Beloved in Christ,

 hope I can say with the holy apostle that you are, by me, dearly beloved, *my joy and my crown*. Yea, you are my honour and in you I would rejoice, being the ornament of my poor ministry, by which the most of you have, through the blessing of God, been converted to Jesus Christ. And if you stand fast in the faith, in one Spirit, striving together for the faith of the gospel, and do adorn your profession, living in love, and endeavouring to keep the unity of the Spirit in the bond of peace, you will cause my latter days to be most sweet and comfortable to me after all those troubles, sorrows, and reproaches I have met with, both from within and from without. Evident, it is, God hath most eminently appeared to strengthen your hands. Though the archers have sorely grieved you, and shot at you, yet your bow abideth in strength, and that the arms of your hands may still abide strong by the arm of the mighty God of Jacob, shall be my continual prayers.

My brethren, I here present you with that which you have so long waited for and desired me to endeavour to do, namely to state an account of the most concerning articles of your faith, which you have heard read, and have approved of, and which I thought good no longer to delay the doing of.

1. Not knowing how soon I may put off this tabernacle, and therefore would leave behind me an account of that holy doctrine and order in which, through grace, you are established, for at your desire also I have drawn up the whole rules of your holy discipline, which you may have added unto this, and bound up together.

2. And the rather I have done this because the general and more large confession of the faith of our churches is now out of print. But that is not all, for that being *12d.* price, some cannot well purchase it.

3. And also that all men may see what our faith is, and that we differ not from our brethren who bear other names in any fundamental point or article of faith, and that they may discern the difference between you and some that bear the same name with you.

4. Though you agree in the general with all other churches of the same faith in all those articles there inserted, yet therein your whole faith is not comprehended, namely that of imposition of hands upon baptized believers as such, and singing of God's praise, etc., because some of our churches dissent from us therein. Yet, my desire is you would nevertheless shew all tenderness, charity and moderation to such as differ from you in those cases, and not refuse communion with them. And, indeed, your late sweet temper appears to be such that I need not press you to this.

All that I shall say more is to entreat you to labour after holiness, and to awake out of sleep that you may adorn your sacred profession and prepare to meet the Lord, that as you have a good doctrine, you may also have a holy and good conversation, and then we need not fear who can harm us whilst we are followers of that which is good. O let us bear one with another. And if in anything we differ, let us avoid all animosities.

Brethren, great things are near. Watch and pray; look out and be ready. But at present, I shall conclude with the words of the apostle. "Finally, brethren, farewell. Be perfect, be of good comfort, be of one mind, live in peace; and the God of love and peace shall be with you."[1]

So prays your unworthy brother, pastor, overseer, and servant, who earnestly desires your prayers also,

BENJAMIN KEACH
From my house in Freemans-lane
by Horsleydown, Southwark.
August 16, 1697

---

[1] [2 Cor. 13:11.]

That the following articles contain what the foresaid church believes concerning those truths asserted therein, we, whose names are hereunto subscribed, do testify in the name and by the appointment of the whole congregation, the 10th day of the 6th month, commonly called August, 1697.

Benjamin Keach, pastor
Benjamin Stinton, teacher
John Roberts, deacon
Edward Foley, deacon
Joshua Farrow, deacon
Thomas Stinton, deacon
John Valley, deacon
Isaac Ballard, deacon
John Hoar, Sr.
Edward Newbury
Thomas Turner
John Seamor
Ephraim Wilcocks
James Wilmott
Daniel Dines
Richard Thoubals
John Weston
John Clark
Thomas Ayers
John York
George Starkey, Sr.
Benjamin Harris
George Starkey, Jr.
John Beavis
Thomas Hill
Joseph Berry
William Farmworth
Joseph Jennings
John Fowle, Sr.
Thomas Fowle
John Fowle, Jr.

Henry Skeer
John Greensmith
Jeremiah Lions
William Putman
Nath. Holden
William Cattrel
Thomas Harvey
Thomas Richford
Joseph Worley
Peter Carter
William Forister
Sam Cox
John Sparke
James King
William Deale
Simon Agars
John Hoar, Jr.
Thomas Gunning
William Mais

The Articles of Faith

Of God, and of the Holy Trinity

I. We do believe, declare, and testify that there is but one only living and true God, who is a spirit infinite, eternal, immense and unchangeable in his being, wisdom, power, holiness, justice, goodness, truth and faithfulness.[1]

II. That there are three persons in the Godhead, the Father, the Son, and Holy Spirit,[2] and that these three are one God,[3] the same in essence, equal in power and glory.

Of the Decrees of God

III. That the decrees of God are his eternal purpose, according to the counsel of his will,[4] whereby for his own glory he hath foreordained whatsoever comes to pass,[5] even those evils that his wisdom and justice permits for the manifestation of the glory of those his attributes, and that God executes his decrees in the

---

[1] John 4:24; Job 11:7–9; Psa. 90:2; Jas. 1:17; Exod. 3:4; Rev. 4:8; Deut. 6:4; Exod. 34:6–7.

[2] Matt. 28:19.

[3] 1 John 5:5.

[4] Eph. 1:4, 11.

[5] Rom. 9:22–23.

works of creation and providence.

Of Creation

IV. That the works of creation are God's creating all things of nothing by his word of power,[6] in six days, and all very good. That God created man male and female,[7] after his own image, in knowledge, righteousness, and holiness, with power and dominion over the creatures.

Of God's Providence

V. We believe that God's works of providence are his most holy, wise, and powerful preserving, and governing all his creatures, and their actions.

Of the Holy Scriptures

VI. We believe the holy Scriptures of the Old and New Testament are the word of God, and are the only rule of faith and practice,[8] all things being contained therein that are necessary for us to know concerning God and our duty unto him, and also unto all men. That all persons ought to read, hear, and understand the holy Scriptures. That the light of nature and works of providence, though they declare plainly there is a God, yet not so effectually as the holy Scriptures, nor can we know without them how, and in what space of time, God created all things.[9] Neither came we

---

[6] Gen. 1; Heb. 11:3.

[7] Gen. 1:26–28; Col. 3:10; Eph. 4:24.

[8] 2 Tim. 3:16; Eph. 2:20; John 5:39; Deut. 17:18; Rev. 1:3; Acts 8:30.

[9] Gen. 1; 3:15–16.

any other ways, but by the holy Scriptures, to the knowledge of Christ, the blessed Mediator,[10] which indeed none can savingly know but by the word and Spirit of God.

Of Original Sin

VII. We do believe that God, having created man, entered into a covenant of life with him upon the condition of perfect obedience, making the first Adam a common head to all his seed.[11] And that our first parents, being left to the freedom of their own will, fell from the estate wherein they were created by eating of the forbidden fruit. And that Adam, being set up as a public person, we all sinned in him and fell with him into a state of sin, of wrath and misery, the sinfulness of which state consists in the guilt of Adam's first sin, the want of original righteousness, and the corruption of our whole nature, from whence all actual sins proceed, as water out of a filthy and an unclean fountain. So that not only by imputation all men became sinners in the first Adam, but also as the same corrupt nature is conveyed to all his posterity, who descend from him in ordinary generation.[12]

By this sin, all mankind lost the image of God and communion with him, being liable to all the miseries of this life, and to death itself, and also are dead in sins and trespasses, and obnoxious to the wrath of God, and the eternal pains of hell for ever.[13]

---

[10] Job 20:30–31; 21:24.

[11] Gen. 3:5–6; 6:5; Ecc. 7:29; Rom. 3:10–14, 23; 5:6, 17; 6:23; 7:7, 14, 17–18, 23–24; 8:7; 1 John 3:4; Tit. 1:13; Jer. 17:9; Jas. 1:14; 1 Cor. 15:14; Col. 1:22; Matt. 15:19; Lam. 3:39; Gal. 3:10.

[12] Job 11:12; 15:14; 25:4.

[13] Col. 3:10; Tit. 1:13; Psa. 51:5.

Hence, we say that all are conceived and born in sin and are the children of wrath,[14] even the elect as well as others, being wholly defiled in all the faculties and parts of soul and body,[15] and utterly indisposed and disabled to do anything that is spiritually good, and wholly inclined, with a strong propensity, to all things that are evil.

Of Man's Free Will

VIII. We believe man, in his state of innocency, had freedom of will to do good. But by the fall he hath utterly lost all that power and ability, being woefully depraved in all the faculties of his soul,[16] there being in the will and mind of all, naturally, much enmity against God,[17] and a total aversion to him, and to everything that is spiritually good,[18] loving darkness and rebelling against the light.

But when a man is renewed by divine grace,[19] though there is no force put upon the will,[20] yet it is made willing and acts freely in the day of God's power, though the work is not perfect in any faculty in the regenerate, nor will be in this life.

---

[14] Eph. 2:2–3.

[15] Gen. 6:5; Rom. 7:5, 14–17, 23–24.

[16] Eph. 2:2–3.

[17] Rom. 8:7.

[18] Job 24:13.

[19] Eph. 4:28.

[20] Col. 1:21; Psa. 110:3; Rom. 7:11, 17–18, 23–24.

Of Christ the Mediator

IX. We believe that God, having out of his own mere good pleasure and infinite love,[21] elected some persons of the lost seed of the first Adam unto everlasting life from all eternity, did enter into a covenant of grace with the second person of the Trinity, who was set up as the common head of all the elect, to deliver them out of the state of sin and misery,[22] and to bring them into a state of salvation and eternal happiness.

That the second person in the Godhead,[23] being the eternal Son of God, coessential, and coequal with the Father, according to that holy covenant and compact that was between them both, became man, or assumed our nature,[24] and so was, and continueth to be, God and man in two distinct natures, in one person forever. And that he, the Son of God, by his becoming man,[25] did take unto him a true body and reasonable soul, being conceived by the Holy Spirit in the womb of the virgin, and was born of her, yet without sin.

Of the Offices of Christ

X. We believe that the Lord Jesus Christ, who is our redeemer and the one blessed mediator between God and man,[26] executeth a threefold office, both the office of a priest, the office of a king,

---

[21] Eph. 1:4; Rom. 3:20–22; Gal. 3:21–22; 1 Tim. 2:5–6; John 1:14; Gal. 4:4.

[22] Rom. 9:5; Luke 1:35; Col. 2:9; Heb. 7:24–25.

[23] Phil. 2:6; Zech. 6:13.

[24] John 1:14; 1 Tim. 2:5; Heb. 2:14.

[25] Matt. 2:26, 38; Luke 1:27, 31, 34–35; [Gal. 4:4–5; Heb. 2:14–18.]

[26] 1 Tim. 2:5.

and the office of a prophet.

First, that he executeth the office of a priest, (1.) In his once offering up himself a sacrifice to satisfy divine justice, and to reconcile God to us, and us to God.[27] (2.) And in making continual intercession for us, that the merits of his blood may be made effectual unto us.[28]

Secondly, that he executeth the office of a king in subduing us unto himself, and in giving us laws and holy precepts, by which we ought to walk, and also in his restraining and conquering all his, and our, enemies.[29]

Thirdly, that he executeth the office of a prophet, in revealing to us, by his word and Spirit, the whole will of God concerning all things that appertain to faith and practice.[30]

Of Christ's Humiliation and Exaltation

XI. We believe that Christ's humiliation consisted in that great condescension of his in assuming our nature,[31] and being born in a low condition,[32] made under the law, undergoing the many miseries of this life, the wrath of God, the curse of the law, and the ignominious death of the cross, continuing under death for a time.

And that his exaltation consisteth in his rising again from the

---

[27] Heb. 2:17; 7:24; Acts 15:14–16.

[28] 1 John 2:2; Heb. 7:25; 9:24; 10:21.

[29] Isa. 32:1–2; 33:22; 1 Cor. 15:25; Psa. 100.

[30] Acts 3:22; John 1:18; 1 Pet. 1:10–12; John 15:15; 20:31.

[31] Gal. 4:4; Heb. 12:23; Isa. 53:2–3; Luke 22:44.

[32] Matt. 27:46; Phil. 2:8; 1 Cor. 15:4; Acts 2:24–27, 31.

dead [on] the third day, and in his ascending up into heaven, in sitting at the right hand of God,[33] angels, powers, and principalities being made subject unto him, and in his being made judge of the quick and dead.

Of Effectual Calling

XII. We do believe that we are made partakers of the redemption purchased by Christ by the effectual application of his merits, etc., unto us by the Holy Spirit, thereby uniting us to Christ in effectual calling.[34] And that effectual calling is the work of God's free grace,[35] who by his Spirit works faith in us, who are altogether passive therein,[36] and convincing us of sin and misery, enlightening our minds in the knowledge of Christ, and renewing our wills, and changing our whole hearts, he doth persuade and enable us to embrace Jesus Christ freely, as he is offered in the gospel.

Of Justification

XIII. We do believe justification is a free act of God's grace,[37] through that redemption which is in Christ, who as our head was acquitted, justified, and discharged, and we in him when he rose from the dead.[38] And when applied to us, we, in our own per-

[33] 1 Cor. 15:4; Mark 16:19; Eph. 1:20; Acts 1:11; 17:31; 1 Pet. 3:22.

[34] John 1:11; Tit. 3:5–6; Eph. 1:13–14; 1 Cor. 1:9; Eph. 2:8.

[35] Eph. 3:17.

[36] 1 Cor. 1:9; 2 Tim. 1:9; 2 Thess. 2:13–14; Acts 2:37; 20:18; Eze. 36:27; John 6:44–45.

[37] Rom. 3:23–26.

[38] Eph. 1:6–7; Tit. 3:7.

sons, are actually justified,[39] in being made and pronounced righteous[40] through the righteousness of Christ imputed to us, and all our sins, past, present, and to come, forever pardoned, which is received by faith alone. And that our sanctification, nor faith itself, is any part of our justification before God, it not being either the habit, or act of believing, or any act of evangelical obedience imputed to us, but Christ and his active and passive obedience only, apprehended by faith.[41] And that faith, in no sense, tends to make Christ's merits more satisfactory unto God, but that he was as fully reconciled and satisfied for his elect in Christ by his death before faith as after,[42] otherwise it would render God only reconcilable,[43] not reconciled, and make faith part of the payment or satisfaction unto God,[44] and so lessen the merits of Christ, as if they were defective or insufficient. Yet, we say, it is by faith that we receive the atonement, or by which means, as an instrument, we come to apprehend and receive him, and to have personal interest in him, and to have our free justification evidenced to our own consciences.

Of Adoption

XIV. We believe adoption is an act of God's free grace,[45]

[39] Rom. 5:15–18.

[40] 1 Cor. 1:30; 2 Cor. 5:21.

[41] Acts 13:39.

[42] 2 Cor. 5:21.

[43] Phil. 3:7–9.

[44] Rom. 10:5.

[45] 1 John 3:1.

whereby such who were the children of wrath by nature are received into the number, and have right to all the privileges of the sons of God.[46] And that such who are adopted are also by the Spirit regenerated, and hence said to be born of God.

Of Sanctification

XV. That sanctification is the work of God's free grace also, whereby we are renewed in the whole man after the image of God, and are enabled more and more to die unto sin and live unto righteousness. And that the benefits we receive, and which flow from or accompany justification, are adoption, sanctification, peace of conscience, manifestations of God's love, joy in the Holy Ghost, an increase of grace, an assurance of eternal life, and final perseverance unto the end.[47]

Of the Souls of Men at Death

XVI. We believe that at death the souls of believers are made perfect in holiness, and do immediately pass into glory, and their bodies, dying in union with Christ or dying in the Lord, do rest in their graves till the resurrection, when they shall be raised up in glory.[48] And that their souls being reunited to their bodies, they shall be openly acknowledged, and acquitted, and made completely blessed, both in soul and body, and shall have the full enjoyment of God to all eternity. And that the souls of the wick-

---

[46] John 1:10; Rom. 8:14; Gal. 2:16; 1 John 3:1–2; 4:7; 5:1.

[47] 2 Thess. 2:13; Eph. 4:13; Rom. 5:1–2, 5; 6:5–7; 8:29–30; 14:17; Prov. 4:18; John 15:3; 1 Pet. 1:5.

[48] 1 Cor. 15:43; Matt. 25:23; 10:32; 1 John 3:2; 1 Cor. 13:12; 1 Thess. 4:17–18; 2 Cor. 5:1; Phil. 1:21–22.

ed, at their death, are cast into hell, or are in torment.[49] And that their bodies lie in the grave under wrath, and shall, by virtue of the power of Christ, be raised from the dead. And their souls being reunited to their bodies, shall be judged and condemned, and cast into a furnace of fire, or into unspeakable torment with the devil and his angels, forever and ever.[50]

Of the Law

XVII. We believe God requires obedience of man, and that the rule of that obedience is the moral law, as it is in the hands of Christ,[51] which teacheth all persons their duty to God and to man. The sum of all being this: to love the Lord our God with all our hearts, with all our souls, and with all our strength, and our neighbours as ourselves. And that though the law is abolished as a covenant of works, and as so considered, we are dead to it and that dead to us,[52] yet it remains as a rule of life and righteousness forever.

XVIII. We believe no mere man, since the fall, is able in this life perfectly to keep the holy law of God, and that every offence against the law deserves eternal death, though some sins are more heinous in God's sight than others.

---

[49] Luke 16:25; 1 Pet. 3:19–20.

[50] Luke 16:23–24; Acts 1:25; 1 Pet. 3:19; Psa. 49:11; John 9:28–29; 2 Thess. 1:8–9.

[51] Mic. 6:8; 1 Sam. 15:22; Rev. 2:14; Matt. 19:17; 22:37–40.

[52] 1 John 3:4; Rom. 7:3–4.

And that God, as a simple act of mercy, will not, *doth* not, pardon any man, neither doth it seem consistent with his holiness and justice so to do without a full Satisfaction.[53] Wherefore he substituted Christ in our room and stead, perfectly to keep the whole law and to die,[54] or bear that wrath which we deserved for our breaking of it,[55] he being pleased, in his infinite love and grace, to transfer our sins, guilt, and punishment, upon his own Son, who took our nature upon him, as our blessed head and representative, that his active obedience and righteousness might be our just title unto eternal life, and his death, who bore our hell-torments, be our full discharge from the wrath of God, and eternal condemnation.[56]

And that all who would receive this title,[57] and have this discharge, so as to escape God's wrath and the curse of the law,[58] must fly to Christ and lay hold on him by faith, which faith is known by its fruits, having lively, sin-killing, soul-humbling,[59] self-abasing, Christ-exalting, and heart-purifying operations always attending it.

---

[53] Exod. 34:6; Rom. 3:25–26.

[54] Gal. 4:4.

[55] Isa. 53:4–6, 10–11; 1 Pet. 2:24.

[56] Rom. 8:1.

[57] John 3:15–16; 5:24.

[58] Heb. 6:18–20; Col. 2:12; Acts 15:9.

[59] Acts 2:36; Job 42:5; 1 Pet. 2:7; John 3:3.

Of Faith and Repentance

XIX. We believe that faith is a saving grace,[60] or the most precious gift of God, and that it is an instrument whereby we receive, take hold of, and wholly rest upon Jesus Christ, as offered to us in the gospel, that repentance unto life is also a saving grace,[61] whereby a sinner, out of a true sense of sin and apprehension of God's mercy in Christ, doth, with grief and hatred of his sins, turn from them. And that though repentance is in order of nature called the first principle of the doctrine of Christ, yet we believe no man can savingly repent unless he believes in Jesus Christ,[62] and apprehends the free pardon and forgiveness of all his sins through the blood of the everlasting covenant, and the sight and sense of God's love in a bleeding Saviour, being that only thing that melts and breaks the stony heart of a poor sinner,[63] as the sight of a free pardon from a prince humbles the stout heart of a rebellious malefactor.

Of the Means of Grace

XX. We believe that the outward and more ordinary means, whereby Christ communicates to us the benefits of redemption, are his holy ordinances,[64] as prayer, the word of God, and preaching, with baptism, and the Lord's Supper, etc., and yet notwith-

---

[60] John 1:12; Isa. 26:3–4; Phil. 3:9; Eph. 2:8.

[61] Acts 2:37; John 2:12; Jer. 3:22; 31:18; Eze. 36:31; 2 Cor. 7:10; Isa. 1:16–17; Heb. 6:1–2.

[62] Zech. 12:10.

[63] Acts 2:36.

[64] Matt. 28:19–20; Acts 2:42, 46–47; Neh. 8:8; 1 Cor. 14:24–25.

standing it is the Spirit of God that maketh prayer,[65] reading, *etc.,* and specially the preaching of the word, effectual to the convincing, converting, building up, and comforting, through faith, all the elect of God unto salvation.

And that it is the duty of all that the word may become effectual to their salvation,[66] to attend upon it with all diligence, preparation, and prayer, that they may receive it with faith and love, and lay it up in their hearts, and practise it in their lives.[67]

Of Baptism

XXI. We believe that baptism is a holy ordinance of Christ, or a pure gospel-institution, and to be unto the party baptized a sign of his fellowship with Christ in his death, burial, and resurrection, and of his being grafted into him, and of remission of sins, and of his giving himself up to God, through Jesus Christ, to walk in newness of life.[68]

We also believe that baptism ought not to be administered to any but to those who actually profess repentance towards God and faith towards our Lord Jesus Christ,[69] that the infants of believers ought not to be baptized, because there is neither precept, or example, or any certain consequence in the holy Scripture for any such practice.[70] And we ought not to be wise above what is

[65] Acts 26:32; Psa. 19:8; Rom. 1:15–16.

[66] Acts 20:32; Rom. 10:13–17; Prov. 8:34.

[67] 1 Pet. 2:1–2; Psa. 119:18; Heb. 4:2; 2 Thess. 2:10; Jas. 1:25.

[68] 1 Pet. 3:21; 1 Cor. 12:13; Matt. 28:19–20; Rom. 6:3–5; Col. 2:12–13; Gal. 3:27; Acts 2:38; 22:16.

[69] Acts 8:37; Col. 2:21–22.

[70] Rev. 22:18; Prov. 30:6.

written. And that a human tradition or custom ought not to be regarded, but that it is sinful, and abominable.

We believe also that baptism is only rightly administered by immersion, or dipping the whole body in water, "into the name of the Father, and of the Son, and of the Holy Spirit,"[71] according to Christ's institution and the practice of the apostles, and not by sprinkling, or pouring of water, or dipping some part of the body in water, after the tradition of men.

And that it is the indispensable duty of such who are baptized to give up themselves to some particular orderly church of Jesus Christ, and to walk in all the commandments and ordinances of the Lord blameless, baptism being an initiating ordinance.[72]

Of a True Church

XXII. We believe a true church of Christ is not national, nor parochial, but doth consist of a number of godly persons, who upon the profession of their faith and repentance have been baptized, and in a solemn manner, have in a holy covenant given themselves up to the Lord, and to one another,[73] to live in love, and to endeavour to "keep the unity of the Spirit in the bond of peace,"[74] among whom the word of God is duly and truly preached,[75] and holy Baptism, the Lord's Supper, and all other ordinances are duly administered, according to the word of God,

---

[71] Matt. 3:16; 28:19–20; John 3:23; Acts 8:38; Rom. 6:3; Col. 2:13.

[72] Acts 2:41–42; 5:13–14; 1 Pet. 2:5; Luke 1:6.

[73] Acts 2:40–42.

[74] Eph. 4:3.

[75] Acts 2:40–46; 1 Cor. 16:1–2.

and the institution of Christ in the primitive church, watching over one another, and communicating to each other's necessities, as becometh saints, living holy lives, as becomes their sacred profession, "and not to forsake the assembling themselves, as the manner of some is,"[76] or to take leave to hear where they please in other places when the church is assembled, but to worship God and feed in that pasture, or with that church, with whom they have covenanted, and given up themselves as particular members thereof.

Of Laying on of Hands

XXIII. We believe that laying on of hand with prayer upon baptized believers, as such, is an ordinance of Christ, and ought to be submitted unto by all such persons that are admitted to partake of the Lord's Supper,[77] and that the end of this ordinance is not for the extraordinary gifts of the Spirit, but for a farther reception of the Holy Spirit of promise, or for the addition of the graces of the Spirit, and the influences thereof, to confirm, strengthen, and comfort them in Christ Jesus,[78] it being ratified and established by the extraordinary gifts of the Spirit in the primitive times to abide in the church, as meeting together on the first day of the week was,[79] that being the day of worship, or Christian Sabbath, under the gospel. And as preaching the word

---

[76] Heb. 10:25.

[77] Heb. 5:12; 6:1–2; Acts 8; 19:6.

[78] Eph. 1:13–14.

[79] Acts 2:1.

was,[80] and as baptism was,[81] and prayer was,[82] and singing Psalms was,[83] so this of laying on of hands was.[84] For as the whole gospel was confirmed by signs and wonders, and divers miracles and gifts of the Holy Ghost in general, so was every ordinance, in like manner, confirmed in particular.[85]

Of the Lord's Supper

XXIV. We believe that the holy ordinance of the Lord's Supper, which he instituted the night before he was betrayed, ought to be observed to the end of the world, and that it consisteth only in breaking of bread and drinking of wine in remembrance of Christ's death, it being appointed for our spiritual nourishment and growth in grace, and as a farther engagement in, and to all duties we owe to Jesus Christ, and as a pledge of his eternal love to us, and as a token of our communion with him, and one with another. And that due preparation and examination is required of all that ought to partake thereof, and that it cannot be neglected by any approved and orderly member without sin.[86]

Of Church Officers

XXV. We do believe that every particular church of Christ is

[80] Acts 10:44.

[81] Matt. 3:16.

[82] Acts 4:31.

[83] Acts 16:25–26.

[84] Acts 8; 19.

[85] Heb. 2:3–4.

[86] Matt. 26:26–28; Mark 14:21–23; Luke 22:19–20; 1 Cor. 11:23–27; Acts 20:17.

independent, and that no one church hath any priority or super-intendency above or over another.[87] And that every church ought to be *organical*, that an elder, or elders, a deacon, or deacons, ought to be elected in every congregation, according to those holy qualifications laid down in the word of God.[88] And that the said elders and deacons so chosen ought solemnly to be ordained with prayer and laying on of hands of the eldership, that such churches as have not officers, so ordained, are disorderly, there being something still wanting.[89]

Of Prayer

XXVI. We believe prayer is a holy ordinance of God, and that it ought to be performed by the help and assistance of the Holy Spirit, and that not only the prayer Christ taught his disciples, but the whole word of God is to be our rule how to pray, and pour forth our souls unto God, and that it is the indispensable duty of all godly families, and others also, as well as private Christians, daily to pray for all things they need, and to give thanks every day for all good things they receive, and that the omission of this duty is a great scandal to religion,[90] and a great evil when it is carelessly or negligently performed.[91]

---

[87] 1 Tim. 3:1–2; Tit. 1:5.

[88] 1 Tim. 3:2–12.

[89] Tit. 1:5–8; Acts 13:3; 1 Tim. 4:14; 5:22.

[90] Jer. 10:25.

[91] Phil. 4:6; Psa. 47:7; 65:2; 1 John 4:23; 1 Pet. 2:5; Rom. 8:26; John 5:14; Ecc. 5:1–2; Jas. 5:16; Eph. 6:18; 1 Cor. 14:14; Col. 4:2; Josh. 24:15; Gen. 18:19.

Of Singing of Psalms

XXVII. We believe that singing the praises of God is a holy ordinance of Christ, and not a part of natural religion, or a moral duty only, but that it is brought under divine institution,[92] it being enjoined on the churches of Christ to sing Psalms, hymns, and spiritual songs,[93] and that the whole church in their public assemblies, as well as private Christians, ought to sing God's praises, according to the best light they have received. Moreover, it was practised in the great representative church by our Lord Jesus Christ with his disciples after he had instituted and celebrated the sacred ordinance of his holy supper, as a commemorative token of redeeming love.[94]

Of the Christian Sabbath

XXVIII. We believe that one day in seven ought to be solemnly observed in the worship of God, and that by Moses's law, the Jews and proselyted strangers were to keep the seventh day.[95] But from the resurrection of Christ, the first day of the week ought by all Christians to be observed holy to the Lord, that being called the Lord's Day.[96] And the first time the church met together after Christ's ascension was on the day of Pentecost, which was the first day of the week, as tradition hath handed it down.[97] And on

---

[92] Eph. 5:19; Col. 3:16.

[93] Acts 16:25; Heb. 2:12; Jas. 5:13.

[94] Matt. 26:30; Mark 14:26.

[95] Exod. 20.

[96] Rev. 1:10.

[97] Acts 2:1–2; 20:7.

that day, the church also met together to break bread, and make collections for the poor saints.[98] And no mention is made that any one gospel-church kept the Jewish Sabbath in all the New Testament. And we believe that an apostolical precedent is equivalent to an apostolical precept in this case.

Of Ministers and Their Maintenance

XXIX. We do believe that every brother that hath received a gift to preach, having first passed the probation of the church, and being regularly called by the same,[99] ought to exercise the said gift to the edification of the church when desired,[100] and that no brother ought to take upon him to preach until he has a lawful call so to do.

Moreover, we believe that it is the indispensable duty of every church, according to their ability, to provide their pastor, or elders, a comfortable maintenance, as God hath ordained that he that preaches the gospel should live of the gospel, and not of his own labour, but that he should wholly give himself up to the work of the ministry, and to watch over the flock, being to be freed from all secular business, and encumbrances of the world.[101] And yet, it is [an] abominable evil for any man to preach the gospel for filthy lucre sake, but he must do it of a ready mind.[102]

---

[98] 1 Cor. 16:2.

[99] 1 Tim. 3:2; Eph. 4:11.

[100] 1 Pet. 4:10; Rom. 12:6–7.

[101] 1 Cor. 9:9–14; Rom. 15:27; Gal. 6:6; 1 Tim. 5:15.

[102] 1 Pet. 5:2.

Of the First Covenant

XXX. We believe that the first covenant, or covenant of works, was primarily made with Adam,[103] and with all mankind in him,[104] by virtue of which he stood in a justified state before the fall,[105] upon the condition of his own perfect and personal obedience. But by the fall he made himself uncapable of life by that covenant.

That the law God gave by Moses to Israel was of the same nature of that given to Adam,[106] being a second ministration of it, but not given for life, but to make sin exceeding sinful, and to shew how unable man was in his fallen state to fulfil the righteousness of God.[107] And so, with the ceremonial law, it was given in subservienty to the gospel, as a schoolmaster to bring sinners to Christ.[108]

Of the New and Second Covenant

XXXI. We believe the covenant of grace was primarily made with the second Adam,[109] and in him with all the elect, who as God-man or mediator, was set up from everlasting as a common person, or as their head and representative,[110] who freely obliged

[103] Gen. 2:17.

[104] Rom. 3:12.

[105] Rom. 5:10–30; 10:5.

[106] Rom. 3:19–20; 2 Cor. 3:9, 11.

[107] Rom. 7:7–13.

[108] Gal. 3:10.

[109] Zech. 6:13.

[110] Rom. 3:23–26; Isa. 57:5–6, 10–11.

or engaged himself to the Father for them, perfectly to keep the whole law in their nature that had sinned,[111] and to satisfy divine justice by bearing their sins upon his own body, that is the guilt of all their sins, which were laid upon him, and that he sustained that wrath and curse in his body and soul that was due to them for all their transgressions. And having received their discharge from wrath and condemnation, he gives it out to all that believe in him and obtain union with him, who are thereby brought actually into the said new covenant, and have a personal right to all the blessings thereof.[112]

Of Election

XXXII. We do believe that God, from all eternity, according unto the most wise and holy counsel of his own will,[113] freely and unchangeably decreed and ordained, for the manifestation of his own glory, some angels and some of the lost sons and daughters of Adam unto eternal life,[114] and that their number is so certain and definite that it cannot be either increased or diminished, and that others are left or passed by under a decree of preterition.[115] And that those of mankind that are predestinated and foreordained are particularly and personally designed unto eternal life,[116] and these God, according to his eternal and immutable

[111] Rom. 8:3; Heb. 9:15–17.

[112] Rom. 6:2; 8:16–18.

[113] Rom. 8:29–31.

[114] Acts 13:48.

[115] Rom. 9:11.

[116] 1 Thess. 4:4–5.

purpose, and good pleasure of his will,[117] did choose in Christ, the head of this flection, unto everlasting glory,[118] of his mere free grace, without any foreseen faith or obedience and perseverance therein, or anything in the creature as a condition or cause moving him thereunto, and all this only to the praise of his own glorious grace.

Of Final Perseverance

XXXIII. We believe all those whom God hath chosen, and who are effectually called, justified, and sanctified in Jesus Christ, can neither totally, nor finally fall away from a state of grace,[119] but shall certainly persevere therein unto the end, and eternally be saved,[120] and this by virtue of their election, or the immutable decree of God, and the unchangeable love of God the Father, and by virtue of their union with Christ, together with his death, resurrection, and intercession, as also from the nature of the covenant of grace, and suretyship of Christ, and through the indwelling of the Holy Spirit, who abideth in them forever.[121]

Of the Resurrection

XXXIV. We believe that the bodies of all men, both the just and unjust, shall rise again at the last day, even the same numerical bodies that die, though the bodies of the saints shall be raised

[117] Eph. 1:3–4, 11.
[118] 2 Thess. 2:13.
[119] Rom. 8:28–31.
[120] John 10:28–29; Rom. 8:32–34; 38–39.
[121] 2 Cor. 6:17.

immortal and incorruptible, and be made like Christ's glorious body, and that the dead in Christ shall rise first.

Of Eternal Judgment

XXXV. We believe that God hath appointed a day in which he will judge the world in righteousness by Jesus Christ,[122] or that there shall be a general day of judgment when all shall stand before the Judgment Seat of Christ,[123] and give an account to him for all things done in this body, and that he will pass an eternal sentence upon all, according as their works shall be.[124]

Of Marriages

XXXVI. We believe marriage is God's holy ordinance,[125] that is to say between one man and one woman,[126] and that no man ought to have more than one wife at once,[127] and that believers that marry should marry in the Lord,[128] or such that are believers, or godly persons, and that those who do otherwise sin greatly in violating God's holy precept,[129] and that ministers as well as others may marry, for "marriage is honourable in all."[130]

[122] Acts 17:31.
[123] 2 Cor. 5:10.
[124] Ecc. 12.
[125] Gen. 3:24.
[126] Matt. 19:5.
[127] 1 Cor. 6:16.
[128] Eph. 5:31.
[129] Rom. 7:4.
[130] Heb. 13:4.

Of Civil Magistrates

XXXVII. We do believe the supreme Lord of heaven and earth hath ordained magistrates for the good of mankind,[131] and that it is our duty in all civil and lawful things to obey them for conscience sake. Nay, and to pray for all that are in authority that under them we may live a godly and peaceable life,[132] and that we ought to "render unto Caesar the things which are Caesar's; and unto God the things that are God's."[133]

Of Lawful Oaths

XXXVIII. We do believe it is lawful to take some oaths before the civil magistrate, an oath of confirmation being to put an end to all strife.[134] Nay, and that it is our duty so to do when lawfully called thereunto, and that those that swear ought to swear in truth, in righteousness, and in judgment.

Of Personal Property

XXXIX. We do believe that every man hath a just and peculiar right and property in his own goods, and that they are not common to others. Yet, we believe that every man is obliged to administer to the poor saints, and to the public interest of God, according to his ability, or as God hath blessed him.[135]

---

[131] Rom. 13:1–3; Tit. 3:1.

[132] 1 Pet. 2:13.

[133] Matt. 22:21.

[134] Exod. 20:7; Jer. 4:2; Gen. 24:2; Neh. 5:12; Heb. 6:16–17.

[135] Exod. 20:17; Acts 5:4; 20:33.

Postscript

There is something contained in the 13th article that may seem to want some explication, in these words, speaking of a man actually and personally justified, that his *sins past, present, and to come are all forgiven*. We believing that if any sins of a justified person were afterwards charged upon him, it must of necessity make a breach in his unalterable and everlasting justification, which is but one act in God. Hence, "there is no condemnation to them which are in Christ Jesus."[136] Yet, I find an able and worthy writer[137] distinguisheth pardon of sin thus,

> 1. Fundamentally in Christ, as a common person of all the elect before faith, which lieth in Christ making full satisfaction for all their sins, meriting faith for them, etc.
> 2. Actual, of all the elect in Christ on believing. This actual pardon being nothing else but the actual possession in their own persons of their fundamental pardon in the person of Christ.

And Dr. Thomas Goodwin speaks to the same purpose, to which I agree. And that this actual pardon of the legal guilt is twofold.

> 1. Formal, of all their sins past, removing their legal guilt.
> 2. Virtual, of all their sins to come, preventing their legal guilt.

Dr. Ames[138] speaks to the same purpose, and many others.

---

[136] Rom. 8:1.

[137] Mr. Thomas Gilbert. [Keach is referencing Thomas Gilbert, *A Learned and Accurate Discourse Concerning the Guilt of Sin, Pardon of that Guilt, and Prayer for that Pardon* (London: Nathan Hiller, 1695).]

[138] [Dr. William Ames (1576-1633), the famous English Puritan. Keach is

I cannot see how a believer should be forever formally justified from all sins past, present, and to come, and yet not formally pardoned.

This author which I have lately met with distinguisheth well between legal guilt and gospel guilt—the first obliging to divine wrath, or eternal punishment, the latter, that is gospel guilt, obliging to gospel, or fatherly chastisement for gospel-sins.[139] Now I see not but that as soon as a believer is personally justified, all his sins, though not yet committed as to legal guilt, or vindictive wrath, that is that guilt that obliges to eternal condemnation, are pardoned for the reason before.

Saith he, "virtual pardon keeps off legal guilt where it would be." To which I reply, if it be kept-off so that it never comes upon believers, then it follows they were actually pardoned before in that respect. Yet, he says, sins cannot be said to be formally pardoned before formally committed, but says, "no guilt can come upon them to condemnation, though new guilt." Yet, no new legal guilt, because always justified. We see no hurt if his terms be admitted.

OBJECTION

What do believers then pray for when they pray for the pardon of sin?

---

referencing his classic work, *The Marrow of Theology.*]

[139] Dr. Ames saith, that not only the sins of a justified person that are past are remitted, but also in some sort these to come (Num. 23:25; John 5:24). Yet, he distinguishes between a formal and virtual pardon. Sins past, says he, are remitted to themselves; sins to come, in the subject or person sinning.

Answer. 1. That God would not chastise them sorely, or afflict them as a father, according to the greatness of their offences.

2. That if his chastening hand is upon us, he would be pleased graciously to remove it.

3. That he would be pleased to clear up to our consciences, or give us the evidence of our pardon through Christ's merits, and that we may know we are complete in Christ, or without spot before the throne in our free justification.

4. Nay, believers are to pray to God to remove that sin from them, saith this worthy author, whose desert of punishment cannot be removed from it, and to spread their sins before the Lord in the highest sense of the deepest demerit of all legal punishment so that they may put the higher accent upon the free grace of God, and estimate upon the full satisfaction of Christ, whereby their persons are so fully freed from all actual obligation to any legal punishment, the whole and utmost whereof their sins deserve.

5. Moreover, that God would continue and never revoke his most gracious pardon till he pronounceth the final sentence of it at the day of judgment, as well this author notes, for a renewed sense and assurance of its grant and continuance. And thus, to pray, saith he, there are both precepts and promises.

FINIS

INDEXES

SCRIPTURE INDEX

GENESIS
1	62
1:26–28	62
2:17	80
3:5–6	63
3:15–16	62
3:24	83
6:5	63, 64
9:22	42
18:19	77
24:2	84

EXODUS
3:4	61
20	78
20:7	84
20:17	84
20:24	39, 45
26:3–6	52
34:6–7	61, 71

LEVITICUS
19:17	32, 52

NUMBERS
12:14	21
22:7	43
23:25	86

DEUTERONOMY
6:4	61
17:18	62
33:8–9	[34]

JOSHUA
24:15	77

1 SAMUEL
15:22	70

1 KINGS
6:7	38

NEHEMIAH
1:2	44
5:12	84
8:8	72

JOB
11:7–9	61
11:12	63
15:14	63
20:30–31	63
21:24	63
24:13	64
25:4	63
42:5	71

PSALMS
15:1, 3	16
19:8	73
22:25	[44]
26:8	44
26:14	46
27:4	45
29:9	44
34:3	46
47:7	77
49:11	70
51:5	63
63:1	34
65:2	77
66:16	2, 11
73:16–17	45
84:1–2	46
84:10	46

87:2	43	51:3	46	**MALACHI**
87:5	45	53:2–11	66, 71	3:16 53
90:2	61	55:3	37	
93:5	39, 52	55:8	52	**MATTHEW**
100	66	57:5–11	80	2:26, 38 65
110:3	43, 64	62:5	52	3:16 74, 76
119:18	73			6:6 46
122:3	52	**JEREMIAH**		10:9–10 8
128:5	46	3:15	4	10:32 69
132:13	44	3:22	72	13:18 25
132:15	45	4:2	84	15:19 63
133:1	32	10:25	46, 77	16:19 [43]
133:3	45	17:9	63	18 14, 17, 31, 36
		20:10	7, 36	18:15–20 18, 20, 31, 34, 39, [43], 45
PROVERBS		31:18	72	19:5 83
1:9	39	50:5	2	19:17 70
4:18	69			22:21 84
6:16	30	**LAMENTATIONS**		22:37–40 70
8:34	46, 73	3:39	63	25:23 69
27:23	4			26:26–28 76
30:6	73	**EZEKIEL**		26:30 78
		16:6, 8	51	27:46 66
ECCLESIASTES		36:27	67	28:19–20 61, 72, 73, 74
4:9–13	47	36:31	72	
5:1–2	77			**MARK**
7:29	63	**HOSEA**		14:21–23 76
12	83	2:23	51	14:26 78
				16:1 34
SONG OF SONGS		**JOEL**		16:19 67
4:12	35	2:16	37	
7:12	34			**LUKE**
		MICAH		1:6 74
ISAIAH		6:8	70	1:27–35 65
1:16–17	72			1:35 65
26:3–4	72	**ZEPHANIAH**		1:74–75 52
28:16	37	2:8	7	16:23–25 70
32:1–2	66			
33:22	66	**ZECHARIAH**		
35	46	6:13	65, 80	
		7:10	36	
		12:10	72	

16:23–25	70		72, 74	20:19	52
22:19–20	76	2:46–47	12, 45,	20:20, 27	4
22:44	66		72, 74	20:31–35	3, 73,
JOHN		3:22	66		84
1:10	69	4:23	32	22:16	73
1:11	67	4:31	76	23:5	43
1:12	72	5:3	32	26:32	73
1:14	65	5:4	84	**ROMANS**	
1:18	66	5:5, 11	21, 32	1:15–16	73
2:12	72	5:11–15	1, 12,	1:29	36
3:3	71		74	1:31	28
3:15–16	71	5:7–10	5	3:10–14, 23	63, 80
3:23	74	6:1–10	5	3:19–22	65, 80
4:24	61	6:6	3	3:23–26	67, 71,
5:14	77	8	75, 76		80
5:24	71, 86	8:14	1	5:1–5	69
5:39	62	8:30	62	5:6, 17	63
6:44–45	67	8:37–38	73, 74	5:10–30	80
9:28–29	70	9:26–27	11, 33	5:15–18	68
10:28–29	82	10:33	37	6:2–5	2, 73,
13:12–17	32	10:44	76		74, 81
13:34	52	11:2–6	11	6:5–7	69
13:35	[39]	11:4–24	2	6:17	1, 27
15:3	69	13:3	77	6:23	63
15:12	52	13:39	68	7:3–4	70, 83
15:15	66	13:48	81	7:7–24	63, 64,
20:31	66	14:27	8		80
		15:9	71	8:1	71, 85
ACTS		15:14–16	66	8:3	81
1:11	67	16:5	13	8:7	63, 64
1:25	70	16:25–26	76, 78	8:14	69
2:1–2	37, 75,	17:31	67, 83	8:16–18	81
	78	18:27	31	8:26	77
2:24–31	66	19	76	8:28–31	69, 81,
2:36–37	67, 71,	19:4–6	1, 75		82
	72	20:7	78	8:32–39	82
2:38	73	20:17–28	9, 76	9:5	65
2:41–44	1, 28,	20:18	67		

9:11	81	13:12	69	3:27	73
9:22–23	61	13:25	34	4:4–5	65, 66, 71
10:5	68, 80	14:14	77	5:1	53
10:13–17	73	14:24–25	72	6:1	52
12:6–7	79	14:33, 38	10	6:2	42, 52
12:8	9	14:40	9, 11	6:4	42
12:15	52–53	15:4	66, 67	6:6	7, 53, 79
13:1–3	84	15:14	63		
13:10	42	15:25	66		
14:17–19	11, 53, 69	15:43	69		
15	52	16:1–2	5, 36, 74, 79		
15:1–2	11	16:9	6		
15:16	53				
15:27	79				
16:1–2	31				
16:17–18	30, 34				

EPHESIANS

1:1–2	1
1:3–4, 11	61, 65, 82
1:6–7	67
1:13–14	67, 75
1:20	67
2:2–3	64
2:8	67, 72
2:12–19	1
2:19–21	2, 39
2:20	62
2:23	52
3:17	67
4:3	32, 39, 53, 74
4:11	79
4:13	69
4:16	52
4:24	62
4:28	64
4:31–32	32, 53
5:2	32
5:19	78
5:31	83
6:4	47
6:18	52, 77

1 CORINTHIANS

1:9	67
1:10	29
1:30	68
3:3	29
3:4	37
4:1–2	3
5	19, 21
5:4–5	14, [21]
5:5–7	39
5:7	15
6:16	83
9:7–8	7
9:9–14	7, 8, 79
9:16–17	3
11:18	29
11:19	22
11:23–27	76
12:13	73
12:14–25	28

2 CORINTHIANS

2:6–7	25
2:16	6
3:9, 11	80
5:1	69
5:10	83
5:18	4
5:19–20	6
5:21	68
6:16	51
6:17	82
7:1	52
7:10	72
7:11	21
8:5	2, 51
8:14	36, 39
9:7–13	53
11:21, 23	7
11:29	52
13:11	[59]

GALATIANS

2:16	69
3:10	63, 80
3:21–22	65

PHILIPPIANS

1:21–22	69
1:27	27, 47
2:3	52
2:6	65
2:8	66
3:7–9	68, 72
4:6	77

COLOSSIANS

1:2, 4, 12	1
1:21	64
1:22	63
2:9	65
2:12–13	71, 73, 74
2:19	2
2:21–22	73
3:10	62, 63
3:16	78
4:2	77
4:3	[5]
4:12	52

1 THESSALONIANS

4:4–5	81
4:17–18	69
5:13	6
5:14–15	4, 52–53
5:25	5

2 THESSALONIANS

1:3–6	13
1:8–9	70
2:10	73
2:13–14	67, 69, 82
3:1	[5]

3:6–15	15–17, 30

1 TIMOTHY

1:19–20	22
2:5–6	65
3	3, 9
3:1–12	3, 43, 77, 79
4:3–5	6
4:12	4
4:14	77
5	25
5:15	79
5:17	7
5:19	36–37
5:21	5
5:22	3, 77
5:24	21
6:4	36
6:11	52

2 TIMOTHY

1:9	67
2:15	3
2:23	30
2:25	34
4:2	4
4:16–18	8

TITUS

1:5–10	3, 9, 77
1:13	63
2:10	27
3:1	84
3:2	39, [40]
3:5–6	67
3:7	67
3:9–10	22, 53

3:11	[22]

HEBREWS

2:3–4	76
2:12	78
2:14–18	65, 66
3:10	53
4:2	73
5:12	75
6:1–3	1, 27, 72, 75
6:16–17	84
6:18–20	71
7:24–25	65, 66
9:15–17	81
9:24	66
10:21	66
10:22–25	17, 28, 29, 52, 53, 75
11:3	62
12:12	52
12:23	66
13:1	32
13:4	83
13:5	7
13:17	2, 7
13:18	5
13:31	52

JAMES

1:14	63
1:17	61
1:25	73
2:4	5
3:14–16	35
5:13	78
5:16	52, 77

1 PETER

1:5	69
1:10–12	66
1:16	39
1:22	52
1:25	43
2:1–2	73
2:4–6	2, 38
2:5	1, 52, 74, 77
2:7	71
2:13	84
2:24	71
3:15	2, 11
3:19–20	70
3:21	73
3:22	67
4:10	79
5:1–2	2, 79
5:3–6	5

2 PETER

1:6–7	52
2:1	22
2:2	33
2:10	43

1 JOHN

2:2	66
3:1–2	68, 69
3:4	63, 70
3:17–18	53
4:7	69
4:23	77
5:1	69
5:5	61

2 JOHN

5, 10	53

3 JOHN

9–10	11, 42

JUDE

3	53
11	43
12	30
19	28, 29, 35
23	21

REVELATION

1:3	62
1:10	78
1:13	45
2:1	43
2:14	70
2–3	45
4:8	61
22:18	73

THE PARTICULAR CLASSICS SERIES

1 *The Glory of a True Church* – BENJAMIN KEACH

2 *Baptism and the Distinction of the Covenants* – THOMAS PATIENT

The Particular Classics Series aims to introduce the laity, pastor, and scholar to the classic works of the Particular Baptists. The works included in the series have been carefully selected to both reflect the best of the literature. It is our hope that these selected works will whet the appetite and summon Baptists to take up and read, to discover our Baptist fathers, and recover a heritage that has been buried for far too long.

www.ingramcontent.com/pod-product-compliance
Lightning Source LLC
Chambersburg PA
CBHW070505100426
42743CB00010B/1764